PRIVATE EYE ANNUAL 2009

EDITED BY IAN HISLOP

"Come on, you lot, smarten yourself up – tourists coming"

Published in Great Britain by
Private Eye Productions Ltd
6 Carlisle Street, London W1D 5BN
www.private-eye.co.uk

© 2009 Pressdram Ltd
ISBN 978-1-901784-51-0
Printed and bound in Great Britain by
Butler Tanner & Dennis, Frome, Somerset
2 4 6 8 10 9 7 5 3 1

PRIVATE EYE ANNUAL 2009

EDITED BY IAN HISLOP

WALL STREET CRASH

Your money is safe as houses

Help!

Mayor **Boris Johnson** writes exclusively for the *Daily Beanograph*

Don't Let's Be Beastly To The Bankers

CRIPES! What's got into everyone all of a sudden having a go at those fellows in the City! Blimey! They're only doing their job – at least the chaps who have still got one!

After all, Britain wouldn't be where it was today if it wasn't for all those bods in suits toiling away with their Blackberries night and day on our behalf! And yet to read some of the lefty brigade sounding off you'd think that these bank johnnies had brought the whole bally economy crashing down on purpose!

Look, I know a lot of bankers, many of them were at school or the Varsity with me, and I have dinner with them most nights. And believe me, you couldn't wish to meet a nicer more decent set of coves anywhere between here and the Equator!

And as for their wives! Phwoarrr! Talk about high-class totty! No wonder old Boris is the first to offer *them* a helping hand in the kitchen while hubby is opening the champers or doing a deal on his mobile!

So I say lay off the bankers of Britain. And the bonkers! Whoops! Time for Boris to potter off down to City Hall to do a spot of running London!

© Barclaytrash 2008.

BANK

JP GIRL

KenPyne

POLLY FILLER
on the credit crunch

Worth every penny to keep a hyperactive five-year-old busy whilst mum slaves away at the coalface, writing columns about cutbacks!

SkyPlusPlus: The Useless Simon says he can't live without his daily fix of James May's Extreme Pipe-smoking on More Dave Gold Extra (with special guests Richard Hammond and Jeremy Clarkson).

Handbags, shoes, etc: Don't even go there.

Ocado Delivery: Ditto.

All other items: Double ditto.

Holidays: P-l-e-a-s-e!

LIKE every working mum performing the high-wire juggling act of career and motherhood, I've been experiencing the chill winds of financial meltdown. We're all feeling the pinch, aren't we? And the credit crunch is putting the broke in Lad-broke Grove!

Simon and I had an emergency crisis meeting in our local Starbucks (we called it a Credit Brunch!) and drew up a list of what were essentials in our life and what we could cut back. So here it is:

Toddler Charlie's School Fees: St Duncetan's Academy For Differently Gifted Children.

SO WE had to face the grim reality. There was only one area of our lives where we could realistically economise. And it would hurt.

Yes, the au-pair would have to take a pay cut. It's hard, but I think Dürtcziip (our new useless girl from Georgia) understood. As I explained to her, "There's no point in you sending money home to your village because it no longer exists."

Polly Filler's amusing new book Life Begins At Thrifty *(Johnson and Pearson) is now available at all good bookstores, price £39.99.*

INSTANT STOCK MARKET ANALYSIS

AN AT-A-GLANCE GUIDE TO THE WORLD'S FINANCIAL STATUS

1. Down Toilet

2. Slight Rally

3. Toilet Again

4. Armageddon

The Large Hadron Collider
An Apology

IN COMMON with all other newspapers, we may have given the impression that we regarded the launching of the Large Hadron Collider as the most important scientific experiment in the history of the world, which would allow us to discover the most closely guarded secrets of the universe. We also may have suggested that there was a concomitant risk of bringing the entire universe to a premature end by creating an all-consuming Black Hole.

Headlines such as "Big Bang To Discover God", "By Tonight We Will Know Everything" and "At 8.31am We Will All Be Dead" may have led readers to suppose that the event in question was in some way interesting and worthy of the enormous coverage that we devoted to it.

We now realise that such a view was profoundly mistaken and are happy to accept that the launch of the Large Hadron Collider in Switzerland was in fact part of a long, complex and extremely tedious scientific story which we do not understand and have no desire to read about.

We apologise unreservedly for any disappointment caused to our readers.

© All Newspapers.

WORLD'S MOST IMPORTANT EXPERIMENT GETS UNDER WAY

by Our Science Staff **Cern Britton**

MILLIONS waited with bated breath to witness what had been described as the most audacious experiment in living history – the relaunch of the Gordon Brown.

Hundreds of billions of pounds have been spent on what they are calling "the Big Bore" as scientists attempt to replicate the exact conditions of all those years ago when New Labour was born.

Brown Hole

Said a spokesman, "It is difficult for the layman to imagine how different the universe looked when Tony Blair walked up Downing Street for the first election, but that is what we are going to do."

As the clock ticked away, excitement mounted until at exactly 8.31 am the switches were thrown and millions of new policies were unleashed into the tunnel – many of them invisible to the naked eye – where they collided with each other and then disappeared.

Said one eyewitness, "It was incredible. I have never seen anything like it. In fact I didn't see anything at all."

Big Whimper

However, a spokesman for the project said that everything had gone according to plan and that there was now dark at the end of the tunnel *(cont. p. 94)*

On Other Pages
Big Bank Experiment Fails

ATTEMPTS to reproduce conditions for economic growth ended in failure yesterday when everyone's money disappeared down a black hole and *(That's enough pieces about the Big Bang, Ed.)*

'Big Bang' Mystery Explained

THE mystery of how the large Hadron Collider broke down only a 200 millionth of a second after it began has been solved according to scientists.

"We now believe that there was what we call a Big Bang and then all the lights went out,' said the projects director, Dr Strabismus of Utrecht.

"We eventually tracked down the cause of the problem and discovered a black hole in the fuse box," he continued. "Apparently, electricians are very hard to find in Switzerland, but we are hoping to get the whole thing going again before the world ends."

Listen Again
Today Programme
Radio 4, Wednesday

HEAR once again the legendary sequence leading up to 8.31 am on September 10th 2008 in which Andrew Marr accelerated to record levels of excitement until he finally exploded and turned into a black hole.

"Now where did I put my memory stick?"

Lines On The Occasion Of Her Majesty The Queen Failing To Thank Me For One Of My Brilliant Poems

by The Poet Laureate
Andrew Motion

It's morning and the rain falls.
Like rain falling in the morning.
I am waiting, waiting, waiting...
But for what?

Inspiration.
Will it come like the rain
Falling out of the sky
As if from nowhere?

It is nearly half-past twelve.
And still nothing comes.

Once the Muse descended
And the words flowed on to the page
Like words flowing on to a page
Or rain falling out of the sky.

But since I took the Laureateship
As we poets call it, I am
Blocked.

Blocked.
Like the drain outside my window
Blocked with leaves.

That's quite good actually.
I might put it in my next poem.

Or maybe I won't.
It's too good for the Queen,
Who has never thanked me properly
For my brilliant poems.

Not even my last one
On the State visit of President Sarkozy
And his wife.

Was it too much to ask?

Not a card, not a note.
Not even an email
Now she has discovered
The Internet.

Here comes the postman now
Coming up the path in the rain.
Plop!
The letter falls on to the mat.
Is it the long-awaited message of
Royal gratitude?

No. It is a subscription offer
From The Spectator.
Three free issues and a chance to
Have dinner with Matthew
D'Ancona For £149.
The rain still falls.

© Andrew Lloyd Motion 2008.

● A podcast of this poem, read by Fiona Bruce, is available at www.whingeingtwit.co.uk

---

ME AND MY SPOON

SARAH PALIN

As someone who could well soon be just a heart-beat away from being President of the United States, can I first of all ask you whether spoons have played an important part in your political career?

I was brought up surrounded by old-fashioned Godfearing American spoons. We used them for every kind of thing – from stirring up elk stew to diggin' our way out of a thirty-foot snowdrift. Mercy, we even used 'em to hit pesky Democrats over the head when they got too uppity and the guns got frozen up.

Do you have any foreign spoons?

I am proud to say that all my spoons are made in America although it says here I have seen a Mexican spoon, a Kuwaiti spoon and a French spoon, though don't ask me to describe them as all foreign spoons look pretty darn the same to me!

Do you feel God has given you these spoons for a purpose?

Yes indeedy-doody. The Good Lord in his wisdom has given us the precious gift of spoons to do his work for him. Like it says in the Good Book, "Blessed are the spoonmakers". Yessiree.

Do you and your family share spoons together in your igloo?

We Inuit-Americans have a saying, "Have I Got Moose For You" and when it is time for dinner the whole Palin clan, Trig and Tractor and little Liverpool, they grab their spoons and thank the Good Lord for giving us oil under the ground and polar bears to barbecue in the summer.

Do you use spoons to play hockey?

No sir. A spoon is too sacred for hitting a puck. I may be a simple hockey mum but I know the difference between a stick and a spoon. God Bless America.

Has anything amusing ever happened to you in connection with a spoon?

I'd say Amen to that.

NEXT WEEK: *Steve Jobs – "Me and my jobs"*

"I'm very sorry for your loss. If it's any consolation, he was delicious"

From The Message Boards

Members of the online community respond to the major issues of the day...

Ed Balls announces child protection legislation

How can anyone take this man seriously? The name says it all. Ed indeed! God help us. **– Brown_out**

The Old Gang have had their chance. Time to end the disastrous "democratic" experiment. **–Sword_of_Truth**

Send nu labour 2 the jungle ☺ Nicola will eat Balls for breakfast ☻ lol! **– Danny_Daz**

put-ing nu labor in charge of child pretection is like put-ing king heron in charge of a nursry school – **Hunny_pot**

wat them animal's done to baby p was barbar-ic 😠 if that mother ever has kid's I hope she never does 😠😠 i am so angry i cant think no more **– Eye_4_an_eye**

I saw baby peas in the supermarket today. They call them petits pois but everyone knows what they are. I was with my kids so I bought the ordinary peas, but it was upsetting and they really shouldn't be selling them at this time. **– Emily**

Agree 1000 persent emerly ☺ an in front of kids 2 young 2 understand 😠 supermarkits = scum 😠😠😠 – **Broken_Britan**

we r all 2 blame **– Darling_Deneyze**

u blamin me u slag? **– Justice_4_ Maddie**

You've been a bit quiet lately Justice. **– Rot_in_hell_Myra**

i warnd u befor u lie-in scumbag. i bin on all the maddie threds every day sinse may 2007. i hope ur kids die. by cot deth not by murder i wuldnt wish that on my wirst enemy. god bless baby p an angel in heven **– Justice_4_Maddie**

evry-one shuld keep there poppys an ware them for baby pee, we can call them pop-pees **– Binny**

I will wear my poppy AND suck my mints **– Murray_Maniac**

Anyone not wearing a poppy comes near my kids I swear ill do time **– Family_man**

7

COMPANY DOESN'T GO BUST SHOCK

by Our Economics Staff

IN A dramatic announcement today a firm gave notice that it had not gone bankrupt had not lost all its shareholders money and had not sacked all its employees.

Financial commentators were amazed at this incredible news and said "it is unbelievable. It is reminiscent of the dark days of the late 1990s when hundreds of firms were not going bust on a regular basis."

SIR CLIFF TOPS CHART AGAIN

by Our Pop Staff **Peter Pan**

SIR Clifford Richard has done it again, releasing yet another chart-topping single. This means that the evergreen Sir Cliff has had a single in the top ten in every decade since the Middle Ages.

His first single, a madrigal entitled, "Our Summer Holy Day Is I-cumen In" (by Sir Clifford de Richard and Ye Shadows), came out in 1337 and remained at number one for the whole of the Hundred Years War.

Sir Clifford last last night said he was delighted that the single "Thank You For A Life Support System" *(contd p 94)*

Those Austrian Election Results Latest

Vienna South

Mr A. Hitler *(Keep Austria Austrian)* 25,374;

Mr M. Mosley *(Conservative Discipline Party)* 24,722;

Admiral Von Trapp *(Sound of Music Party)* 3.

Neo-Fascist Gain.

School news

St Cakes

Crunch Term begins today. There are three boys and one girl in the school. Prince Abdul Rashid Bin Laden (Coutts) is Treasurer of the Sovereign Fund. Pavlova Oligarchski (Barings) is Head of Pipelines. The Headmaster, Mr R.G. Kipling (O.C.), will be taking all classes until further notice. The Run on the Pound will take place on Founders Day, October 9th. The new School Mosque will be opened by the Very Reverend Rabbi Goldsmith (O.C.). Recessions will be on December 1st.

"Anyway, I'll let you get on"

A Taxi Driver writes

EVERY week a well-known cabbie writes on an issue of burning importance.

This week, **Dave Sleet** (Cab No. 999).

Blimey, guv. Did you see about all them cabs bursting into flames? All by themselves? What do they call it – spontaneous combustion? I don't believe it myself. How can a cab suddenly burst into flames? Don't make any sense. Tell you what, is it a bit warm in here or is it just me? That's funny, I can smell smoke – you're not smoking are you guv, it's not allowed no more, we got a sign up there, look – "No Smoking" – hang on, it's coming from under where I'm sitting! Fuck me, the cab's on fire!

NEXT WEEK: No cabs will be available due to unforeseen circumstances.

"They're nice if you dunk them"

SHOCK NEW NEWS

Blair **did** lie about Ecclestone donation and Formula One tobacco advertising

Bears **do** shit in wood

Pope **is** Catholic

Great Political Quotations Of The 20th Century

"I'm a pretty straight sort of lie"
(T. Blair, 1997)

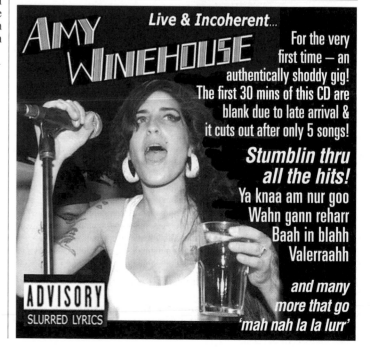

DIARY

DIANA MOSLEY'S A-Z OF FUN AND LAUGHTER

Acton, Harold: For me, no man was ever less like the area of a city associated with his name. Yet for Harold Acton, to be linked with this most unprepossessing part of suburban West London was, I fear, a matter of perpetual ignominy.

Black Shirts: What could be more fun than donning lovely black shirts and then marching with one's head held high through the less, shall we say, "British" areas of the East End?! Whenever my dear husband, Oswald, pursued this passion of his, he and his followers would be greeted by screams of laughter. Or, at any rate, screams. Why quibble? It's so dreadfully small-minded and *spiteful*.

Churchill, Winston: Mr Churchill, as I shall continue to insist upon calling him (since no true patriot ever deemed him deserving of that ill-begotten knighthood) had precious little sense of fun. Otherwise, why on earth would he have pursued his futile little war against the reborn Germany, with its delightful sense of humour and sparkling *get-up-and-go*?

Death Camps: Heaven knows why they were called that when, by all accounts, they were perfectly snug, despite what the busy-bodies may tell us. A lot of nonsense has been written about them. Agreed, they might not have suited people like you or me, and a certain number of unfortunate things may well have come about but, then, they weren't created for us, were they, so who are we to judge? More tea?

Edward VIII: He had an impish sense of fun, and would have made a much better King than his dull old plodder of a brother, who proved so po-faced towards the Fuhrer.

Goebbels, Dr: Josef had a wicked sense of humour. Those who claim he had none are simply showing how spiteful they are. Although he was extremely busy supervising the tremendously impressive economic revival of Germany, he always found time to make one simply HOOT with laughter. For this, I shall always be grateful. By no stretch of the imagination could he be called po-faced.

In addition, Josef was clever, good company, and very well-read. Alas, the pressure of his life got too much for him in the end, and he felt obliged to take his own life, and those of his beloved children. But I feel sure he and his stalwart little wife Magda took the trouble to tell them all a splendid joke before slipping those cyanide pills into their well-brought-up little mouths. Perhaps he told them they were tasty boiled sweets! Josef adored what we used to call a leg-pull!

Hula-Hoop: Magda Goebbels was the master of the Hula-Hoop. Such was the force of her personality that she succeeded in persuading my late husband, Oswald Mosley, to form a crack Hula-Hoop division of his highly-regarded Blackshirts. The division consisted of decent, red-blooded Englishmen proud to proclaim their love of country by marching in formation whilst spinning Hula-Hoops around their waists. Needless to say, that tubby dwarf Churchill loathed the Hula-Hoop, and saw to it that it was the first victim of his absurd rationing.

Italians: I don't know about his war record, and it doesn't particularly interest me, but Benito Mussolini had the most wonderful sense of fun.

Knock-Knock: The Fuhrer simply *adored* "Knock-Knock" jokes. Why, one wonders, are our modish contemporary historians so determined to ignore his coltish wit and love of word-play? Instead, they serve us up with the usual tiresome stream of disobliging references to his so-called "love of power" and "anti-semitism". Little do they seem to realise that he was in fact a terrific supporter of the Jews.

Mickey Mouse: Dear darling Michael was a brilliant talker, whose idiosyncratic voice, with American inflections, amused the listener greatly, and whose characteristic ears never overshadowed his natural wit.

Pogo Sticks: My late husband, Sir Oswald, used to insist that his followers ride about on Pogo Sticks. A great visionary, he saw them as the transport of the future. And so they would have been too, but for Winston.

Quisling, Vidkun: His name is synonymous with fun.

Swastikas: Awfully pretty in the right places.

Umbrellas: Tremendous fun for spearing unpatriotic money-lenders with when they make a hoo-hah.

V for Victory: Winston's wretched gesture proved desperately tiresome and overworked. Small wonder the poor National Socialists grew irritated. Where was his sense of humour?

Xylophone: Name me one Jew who ever played the xylophone well, or even half-well. You see!

Yo-Yo: So very tiresome, the habit it has of, when you throw it away, always insisting upon coming back.

Zulus: My husband, Oswald Mosley, was a great believer in the Zulu. From the mid-1920s on, he campaigned without cease for the Zulu to be admitted to White's Club, with reciprocal rights to The Beefsteak. But – typically! he was blocked at every turn by that jealous pygmy Winston.

As told to CRAIG BROWN

Mr David Miliband
An Apology

IN RECENT weeks we may have given the impression that we considered the Foreign Secretary, Mr David Miliband, as the only possible successor to Gordon Brown as leader of the Labour Party and Britain's Prime Minister. We may have inadvertently portrayed Mr Miliband as an extraordinarily gifted politician possessed of a first-rate intellect and gifted with immense charisma. Headlines such as "Step Down Now Gordy And Make Way For Dazzling Dave!" may have led our readers to believe that we in some way entertained a high opinion of Mr Miliband's talents and prospects.

In the light of a photograph of Mr Miliband holding a banana and wearing an inane grin following a conference speech of unparalleled vacuity, we now realise that there was not a jot or scintilla of truth in any of the above.

We further accept that Mr Miliband is a pathetic nincompoop and a prating nitwit and the idea that he should be Prime Minister is as ludicrous as it would be to hand over the premiership to Mr Bean.

We apologise unreservedly to Mr Miliband and have agreed never to refer to him again in any context whatsoever.

© All Newspapers.

The Eye's Most Commented On Web Stories

1. Is Britney Spears John Lennon's love child?

2. Who is Swansea's lesbian cellar murderer?

3. Can pomegranate juice bring back the magic to your love life?

4. "Sex-change ref asked me to marry him" says Lamps.

5. "Is the EU to blame for Global Warming?" asks Dr Barkworth.

Would you like to comment on the most commented stories? Just go to desperatedrivel@telegraph.co.uk

POETRY CORNER

In Memoriam
Reg Varney: actor

So. Farewell Then
Reg Varney.

Star of long-running sitcom
Classic, On.
The Buses

Now your bus has reached
Its terminus
I wonder – is there room
For "one more upstairs"?

      E.J. Thribb (17B –
      Night Bus only)

Also In Memoriam
Jack Scott: weather forecaster

So. Farewell Then
Jack Scott.
You were the first professional

TV weatherman.
You placed magnetic symbols
Of clouds, sun and rain

On a board
And then quite often
They fell off.

Now the sun has gone in
And there is widespread
Depression
Across the country

      E.J. Thribb (17½ ° F)

In Memoriam Sir Clement
Freud: Liberal MP, grandson
of Sigmund Freud, dog food
commercial star, *bon viveur*
and panellist on *Just a Minute*

So. Farewell
Then Sir Clement
Freud.

Liberal MP,
Grandson of
Sigmund Freud,
Dog food commercial
Star, *bon viveur*
And panellist on
Just a Minute.

B-z-z-z-z-z!
"Repetition!"

Yes. That was
Your catchphrase.

And now you
Have no time
Left.

      E.J. Thribb (17½ seconds left)

UK TO BE SOLD TO FRENCH

'A good deal for Britain' says Brown

by Our Electricity Staff **Conrad Black-Out**

THE United Kingdom is to be sold to a French company EBF (Everything Belongs to France) which is wholly owned by the French Government for the sum of £12.52.

Grid is Good

After long negotiations the Managing Director of EBF, Monsieur Mangetout, emerged to tell reporters "From now on the future of Britain is secure and we can guarantee that it will be very much better run than it has been in recent years by a succession of Tory and Labour governments."

He concluded, "All British Power will now be transferred to France."

HOW THAT DEAL STACKS UP

What the French Get
- The remains of British Industry

What the British Get
- £12.52
- Very expensive energy

That Controversial Paul McCartney Israeli Playlist In Full

- Hey Judas Macabeus ♪
- Avocado Fields Forever
- We Can't Work It Out
- Don't Let It Be
- Shekel Lane ♪
- Give War A Chance
- Die and Let Die
- The Long and Winding Wall
- I Want To Hold Your Land

(That's enough hits. Ed)

New From K-Tel Aviv Records

SAATCHI'S EGG DIET LATEST

"I'm very big in the fart world"

"We do prefer the clothes off the body"

'ARCHBISHOP WAS RIGHT' Claims Marx

by Our Religious Affairs Staff **St Francis of Wheen**

ONE MAN with a beard yesterday rushed to the support of another man with a beard in attacking the greed and folly of world capitalism.

Said Karl Marx, 183, speaking from Highgate Cemetery, "I have read the Archbishop of Canterbury's critique of the present international financial crisis – and whilst I don't go along with all that religious stuff, believing as I do that it is similar to a Class A drug – the Archbishop is spot on when he says that these bankers should be strung up. It's the only language they understand."

RELIGIOUS LEADER CRITICISED

by Our Money-lending Correspondent **Phil Church**

BUSINESS leaders have described as "highly inappropriate and naïve" comments made by Jesus yesterday.

"For Jesus to demand that the money lenders get out of his father's temple shows a disturbing lack of understanding of how important the City is," said a leading Pharisee. "Hundreds of thousands of jobs rely on these traders in the City and the wealth they create.

"Jesus would be well advised to check his facts properly, before he starts making such sweeping generalisations in the future.

"I would say his silly outburst rules out his suitability for any form of high office."

Jesus is 2008.

GLENDA SLAGG
Fleet Street's toxic, sub-prime hackette!

■ HATS OFF to Ant and Dec, our brave boys from Toon Town (that's Birmingham, stoopid!?!), who've gone to cheer up the troops in Afghanistan!?!! They're not content to sit around safely in a TV studio fiddlin' the phone lines!?! No sirree!?! When the trumpet sounds, the cheeky chappies Tank and Jet (Geddit?!) will risk their lives bringing mirth to our heroes on the front line!?! Come on, Your Majesty, give them a VC (that's *Very Courageous*, geddit?)!!?!

■ SPARE a thought for our gallant lads on the front line in faraway Afghanistan!?! Each day they risk their lives dodgin' the bullets of the terrible Taliban. And, as if things weren't bad enough, they've now got Ant and Dec to hide from!?!! Talk about the Telly Ban (Geddit?)!?!! Come on, Your Majesty, put them in the Tower of London where they belong!?!!

■ SPARE a thought for poor Mr Nigella (that's Charles Saatchi I'm talkin' about, stoopid!?!). You know why he eats nothing but eggs all day? So he doesn't have to force down the so-called Domestic Goddess's god-awful grub!?! Cream-Fried Chocolate Monkfish with Banana Sorbet, anyone?!??

■ CHARLES SAATCHI!?! What a plonker!?!! Fancy guzzlin' boiled eggs all day when you could be tuckin' in to Nigella's succulent Cream-Fried Chocolate Monkfish with Banana Sorbet!?!! Mmmmm!?! Yum!! Yum!!?!

■ HERE THEY ARE – Glenda's Credit Crunch Cuties!?!

● **Hank Paulson.** George Bush's Money Maestro!?! You can bail *me* out and squeeze my credit any time, Mr Hanky-Panky!??! (Geddit?!)

● **Robert Peston.** The BBC's Scoopmeister!?! OK, so he talks in a silly way and you can't understand a word he says!?! It's not *talk* I'm after?!?? Geddit?!?

● **Vince Cable.** OK, so he's bald and a Lib Dem!? You can't have everything!?!!

Byeee!!

11

COULD NEASDEN GO UNDER?

by Our Credit Crunch Staff **Paul Footsie**

A **LONDON** council, it was learned last night, could well disappear after investing £700 million in the little known Bank of the Antarctic.

Said council leader Fred Dimwit, "This has come as a terrible shock to all those of us who work in the borough. It looked such a good idea when Michele in accounts saw the advert on the internet offering us 28% over six months."

Frozen assets

But now it turns out that the Bank of the Antarctic has literally been affected by a meltdown. The bank's headquarters, Igloo Number Five on the Captain Scott Industrial Estate, is now nothing more than a pool of water owing to global warming.

Neasden ratepayers (Sid and Doris Bankers) were shocked to discover that their borough's assets had vanished along with the ice.

Said Sid, "We now face an uncertain future. We shall have to empty our own wheelie bins and fine ourselves for putting them out on a Tuesday instead of a Wednesday."

Last night Dimwit defended his council's decision to place all its funds with the Bank of the Antarctic.

Polar Bear Market

"How were we to know that it was run by an Inuit and two penguins with no financial experience?"

The advert that lost Neasden £700 million

Top bank bargains today	
The EasyKash Bank of Kazakhstan	18.6% per annum
The Tali Bank of Afghanistan	22.2% per annum
The Bank of Antarctica	28% per six months
The Bank of Zimbabwe	10,600,000% per day

What You Missed

Jim Naughtie: And now for an update on the financial situation, it's over to the BBC's Business Editor, Robert Peston. Robert, what's happening in the markets?

Robert Peston: Aaargh... aaargh... Jim... aaargh... raPIDly changING scenario... aaargh, aaargh... Libor... recapitaliSATion... rumpelstiltskin stannahstairlift.... aargh... aaargh... wider perspective... urgent measures in place... aaargh... leverage... seCURItisation... creDIT default swap... further stock market COLLapse... aargh...

Jim Naughtie: And would you say that this means the collapse of the entire British banking system and we should all queue round the block outside our banks, as we did when you told us about Northern Rock?

Robert Peston: Aargh... Difficult TO predict... hobgoblin... FSA... Bank of England... triparTITE inTERvention...

Jim Naughtie: Thank you, Bob. And now, thought for the day with the Governor of the Bank of England, Rev. Mervyn King – "These days I think all of us wonder from time to time. What the hell's going on? How are we going to get out of this mess? But you know, in a real sense, none of us has a clue *(cont. 94 kHz)*

An Apology

IN RECENT years, we may have given the mistaken impression that the City was the driving force for growth in the economy, and that the "masters of the universe" and "superwomen" in the City who raked in well-earned mega-bonuses for deals which had transformed London into the banking capital of the world were people everyone should be proud of, as the wealth they've created has benefited each and every one of us in some way.

We now realise, in the wake of the ongoing credit crisis, that nothing could be further from the truth, and that the City is in fact nothing but a collection of sharp-suited robber barons, crooks, spivs and peroxide blonde harpies, all shamelessly feeding at the trough as they scoop up mega-bonuses for dodgy deals which have taken us to the brink of Armageddon, and who are deserving of nothing but stoning or beheading for the misery they've wrought.

We apologise for any confusion caused, and any confusion in the future when we criticise the Government's plan to take a share in the banks, saying that stifling risk-taking in the City will only make us all poorer in the long... etc, etc, etc

"Thank God I put all my money into drink"

Credit Crunch Left You Feeling Gloomy? Try The Eye's Ten Ways To Cheer Yourself Up – And They Are All Free!

① Sit in the garden and watch the leaves turn yellow!

② Have a glass of water. The perfect detox!

③ Pop into your attic and see what's there! Hours of fun.

④ Have a good sit down. You've earned it!

⑤ Talk to yourself. It's nice to have someone to listen to you!

⑥ Have a look at the clock and see what time it is. Incredible how time flies!

⑦ Go to the toilet. You'll feel better for it.

⑧ Have a good scratch. Doesn't that feel good?

(That's enough. Ed.)

Have you got a favourite beating-the-credit-crunch-blues tip? Share it with us on pathericrubbish@allnewspapers.com

EYE MONEY

Our team of experts answer your credit crunch queries

Question: Two years ago I opened a flexi-access High Yield Three Year Interest Bond at the Liberian Bank of Commerce. I then converted this bond into a Seven Year Tax Free Non Refundable ISA at the Isle of Man Save and Prosper Building Society. If I were to withdraw my money before the yield window, would my standard rate fixed return be affected by the new regulations regarding offshore credit?

Answer: This is an interesting one. The answer is both yes and no. The key factor which the questioner has not told us is at what rate the stipulated interest was fixed? Was it zero interest because that is what the question raises *(That's enough advice, Ed)*

Let us know your money worries. Our experts are on hand 24/7 to answer your call *(Calls charged at £1.50 per second, minimum duration 10 minutes)*

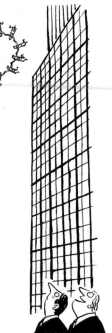

"You've got to hand it to Acme Investments, they have always had style"

EXCLUSIVE TO ALL NEWSPAPERS

DISASTER AS OIL PRICES RISE/DROP

THERE were fresh fears expressed today for the health of the global economy after a sharp fall/rise in oil prices overnight.

The fact that oil prices are falling at an unprecedented rate/rising at an unprecedented rate means it is almost certain that the world will be plunged into a second great depression.

Oil analysts say that unless Opec steps in with decisive action that means oil prices stop falling/rising and start rising/falling the world is doomed.

££££££££££££££££££££££££££££££

HOW TO BEAT THE CREDIT CRUNCH

TOP TEN TIPS

 By Our Entire Staff

① Save on heating bills by buying lots of extra clothes to keep warm.

② Save on your clothing bills by wearing less and turning up the heating.

③ Save on hot water by taking your washing up into the bath and doing it there.

④ Don't serve expensive French wine at your dinner parties – try Ribena with meths. Tastes as good as vintage Margaux!

⑤ Save on lighting bills by going to bed as soon as it's dark. And don't get up again until it's light.

⑥ Save on petrol by never driving faster than 10mph.

⑦ Turn your spare bedroom into an indoor allotment. You can grow a wide range of nutritious vegetables, including mushrooms, lima beans and corn on the cob. And if it's big enough, why not keep chickens or a goat? Remember, the average spare room can feed a family of 15 for a year.

⑧ Forget madcap schemes of grow-your-own-self-sufficiency. Shop around in your local supermarket for past-their-sell-by-date-bargains. It's much cheaper.

⑨ Save on expensive postage. Be your own postman. Simply hop in the car and speed off to deliver that birthday card to your aunt in Glasgow.

⑩ Save pounds by not buying newspapers full of drivel like this, especially not the Telegraph now it's gone up to 90p.

££££££££££££££££££££££££££££££

THE ROYAL BANK OF GNOME

THE Royal Bank of Gnome has been taken over as of this morning by the Government.

I welcome this development and I am happy to give a reassurance to members of my family that my money is perfectly safe.

Despite my sadness at leaving a bank that I have done so much for over the years, I can walk away with the knowledge that I have done everything in my power to safeguard my salary, bonuses and pension scheme. Investors may take comfort in the knowledge that although they have lost all their money, I haven't.

LORD FRED GNOMEWIN
(Formerly Royal Bank of Gnome [RBG]
Now National Bank of Gnome [NBG])

"Your money is safe in my safe"

"If you don't believe in banks, they die"

THE EYE CELEBRATES 100 YEARS OF *007⁻* BOND *007⁻*

Which is the best Bond girl ever? *You choose*

Mixi Mitosis who played Yummy Puss in *GoldenWonder* (1969)

Lois Bacardi who played Honey Trapp in *You Only Die On Sunday* (1973)

Tuesday Polanski who played Randy Lovechest in *Die And Don't Live* (1988)

Amanda Wheatcroft who played Eva Beaver in *Thunderbox* (1981)

Chantelle Mitterrand who played Venus Flytrap in *Yesterday Is Tomorrow* (1993)

Suki Fuki who played Bang Bang in *The Bullet Never Lies* (2001)

Olga Smirnoff who plays Anna Legova in the most recent Bond outing, *You'll Only See This Once* (2008)

(That's enough Bond girls, Ed)

Now Try Our Bond Trivia Quiz

1. What car did Bond drive in the 1972 film *At Her Majesty's Secret Service?* Was it:
a) *Aston Martin DB10b?*
b) *Nissan Sudoku GTI?*
c) *Rolex Oyster Supermariner 713?*

2. Who played gadget boffin Q in the first 17 Bond films? Was it:
a) *Sir John Gielgud?*
b) *Sir Jonathan Miller?*

c) *Michael Fish?*

3. What cocktail does Bond order in the bar at Key Largo in *Moonwalker* (1967)? Is it:
a) *Harvey Headbanger?*
b) *Pink Geranium?*
c) *Manhattan Trouserpress?*
d) *Rolex Aston Martin?*

(That's enough quiz, Ed.)

"Ah, Mr Bond... I wasn't expecting you"

"There's always one"

DE MENEZES INQUEST

'WE DID NOTHING WRONG' Top Policewoman Spells It Out

by Our Court Staff **Karl Marksman**

A DEFIANT Chief Inspector Cressida Knacker told a crowded inquest yesterday that the Menezes killing "was a flawless police operation in which no mistakes were made".

She continued, as weeping relatives were led out of the court, "The fact that an innocent man was shot dead is neither here nor there. And anyway he was acting in a funny way and deserved to be killed."

When asked the question by Michael Hugefeeld QC, "What led you to believe that Mr Menezes was the wanted terrorist?" She answered, "Because our officers thought he was. And anyway he looked just like the photographs that they hadn't seen."

Mr Hugefeeld then asked the Police Chief if this tragedy could happen again.

"Most certainly," she said, "especially if I am in charge. Innocent people will inevitably be killed if we are to avoid innocent people being killed."

Mayor Boris Johnson Tells It Like It Isn't

CRIPES! Everyone is going around saying that I sacked Sir Ian Blair and I'm a total rotter! Well, hang on there, old bean! As I was telling John Humphrys on the Today programme (when he let old Boris get a word in edgeways), I did no such thing! I've always rated superplod Blair and I told him that he was doing a damn good job! Crime down, picaninnies with knives safely behind bars, everything tickety-boo in the capital, what? And blow me down, in walks Brother Blair to my office and says, "Permission to resign, sir". What's a chap supposed to do? I pleaded with him to stay on. I said, "You're fired". Whoops! Old Boris has let the cat out of the bag. Blimey!

© *The Daily Beanograph*

POLICE HUNT FOR NEW CHIEF

by Our Man At New Scotland Yard **Phil Position**

THE Metropolitan Police were last night urgently looking for a new Commissioner.

A spokesman issued a description of the wanted man: "He is a supremely capable, intelligent, far-sighted, middle-aged man with extensive experience of policing at a national level."

He continued, "What we will probably get is a young Brazilian electrician who *(cont. p. 94)*

BROWN 'RECALLS' MANDELSON

I recall that I hate you

The Coat Of Arms Of Baron Mandelson of Malfoy and Hartlepool

PUGNATOR SUM·NON QUITTUS

THE shield is quartered to show the symbols of Lord Mandelson's career. The first quarter commemorates the highly successful Millennium Dome. The second shows a field of moustaches rampant. The third shows heraldic Brussels Sprouts on a background of gravy, and the fourth shows a mortgage from the Britannia Building Society supported by a secret loan from Lord Robinson of Sleaze. The Mandelson motto is underneath and is not, as originally suggested, *Salve Nauticus*!

❝He's not the Prince of Darkness: he's a total poppet❞

Gill Hornby
Notebook

DON'T be taken in by all the talk about a "crazy megalomaniac intent on world domination".

I know Adolf very well because he was a house guest of ours for over six weeks.

And a kinder, more compassionate soul you couldn't wish to meet.

Here are some things you may not know about Adolf:

1. He loves to help with the washing up.

2. He adores dogs.

3. He's happiest when joining in a sing-song. His favourite is the Horst Wessel song.

4. He has beautiful manners. *(That's enough things we don't know. Ed.)*

DAILY not-in-the Mirror
Friday, October 17, 2008

THE MAN THEY CAN'T KILL IS BACK AGAIN

by Our Transylvania Political Staff
Michael Bite

YOU just can't write him off! Every time you think he is dead, you turn round to find he's behind you, smiling and showing off his teeth.

Yes, controversial Vlad Draculson is returning to the Transylvanian Government for the third time and to pave the way for his appointment he has been given a title. So from now on it's Count Dracula, Secretary of State for the Stakeholder Economy and the Blood Banking sector.

Dead Mandy Walking

Said one political observer, "Vlad may not be popular amongst local virgins and frightened village folk but you have to admit that he is a safe pair of fangs."

Batty Decision

Draculson was originally written off as a political force when he was exposed to daylight and quit the world of the living. But he defied expectations and returned to life after only a few hundred years lying low in the crypt.

He then suffered a second setback when he received a stake through the heart and had his head sawn off by opposition leader Van Helsing.

However his third re-awakening is perhaps the most surprising of all. Said one critic, "Count Mandelson is a real pain in the neck *(continued forever)*

Yes! It's Guy Ritchie Mockney Rhyming Slang!

Madonna	Marriage a goner
Bugs Bunny	Who gets the money?
Rub-a-dub-dub	Too much time in the pub
Apples and pears	Malawi air fares
Barnet Fair	Another au-pair
Frog and toad	Wife always on the road
Whistle and flute	Divorce suit
Jack Tar	Had enough Kaball-ah
Dustbin lids	Who gets the kids?
Pony and trap	Films poorly received

NOT A PENNY FOR THE GUY

RGJ

Bullingdon revisited

WHO are they, the magic circle of bright young men from Oxford who now form the nucleus of the modern Conservative Party? From right to far right:

❶ **Nat "Pratt" Rothschild:** Son of Lord Ephraim Rothschild, nephew of Lady Victoria Starborgling de Rothschild, not to be confused with his cousin Lady Vittoria Starborgling di Rothschildi or his second cousin twice removed La Comtesse de Mouton-Rothschild, Premier Cru 1923, serve at room temperature, ideal with game and cheese. Now on sale at Asda at £4.99 – Offer of the Month.

❷ **Cosmo Ricketson-Smythe:** Younger brother of Prince Harry's best friend Rupert "Legless" Ricketson-Smythe. Owns "Cosmo's", the trendy Tangier nightclub, in partnership with Sebastian Cholmondely-Flyte (see below). Old Etonian and close confidant and family friend of David and Samantha Cameron.

❸ **Lord William (Billy) de Winceyette:** Younger son of the Marquess of Bilgewater. Deals in fine art at Vronski and Warminster of Bond Street. Old Etonian who runs fundraising dinners for the Tories in the North West.

❹ **Sir Algy Bunce (Bt):** Racehorse trainer, son of the legendary Archie Bunce, the former chief steward at Newmarket. He is 179th on the Forbes Rich List and advises the Conservative Party on which horse to back in the 4.30. Old Etonian.

❺ **Algernon ffitch-Stoat-Corby:** Scion of the Corby trouser-press dynasty. Runs US hedge fund Forceps Brothers and is estimated to have a personal fortune of £800 billion. Old Etonian and deputy vice-treasurer of the Conservative Leadership Group

❻ **Harry Mount:** Old Etonian, son of Sir Ferdinand Mount, Lady Thatcher's policy advisor. His initiation into "The Buller" involved being rolled down a hill in a portable lavatory. Mount later wrote the best-selling Latin Primer *Portaloo, Portalas, Portalamus, Portalasshole.*

❼ **George "Georgie" Osborne:** Former shadow chancellor and currently garden furniture editor of *Standpoint* magazine, the Conservative quarterly run by wealthy Saudi Old Etonian Prince Abdul Bin-Laden-Twisk *(see above).* Not an old Etonian but allowed in anyway "because we've got to have the odd oik." *(That's enough magic circle. Ed.)*

WHAT THE RUSSIAN OLIGARCH REALLY SAID TO LORD MANDELSON

Hello sailor

The Letter That Left Osborne's Career In Ruins

Sir, Normally I would not dream of writing a letter to the newspapers but I am so shocked by the recent behaviour of one of my summer guests at my villa in Corfu that I have decided to break the habit of a lifetime.

I am referring to the infamous conduct of my very much ex-friend the Rt Hon George Osborne. I realise that times have changed but some of us like to think that there is still a code amongst gentlemen. What took place in and around my villa last September was private and should concern no one except those involved, which is why I am writing to tell your readers and indeed the world exactly what happened.

Osborne, like the total cad that he is, came back to England and blabbed to some ghastly journalist that his fellow guest, my very good friend Peter Mandelson (who, although he bats for the other side, is a thoroughly decent fellow) was being far from flattering in his personal references to the Prime Minister. It was unforgivable of Osborne to pass on this tittle-tattle which he had only heard in the strictest confidence over brandy and cigars at the villa.

This wretched bounder then made it worse by further revealing that Lord Mandelson had been for drinks on the yacht *Chernobyl II* owned by yet another of my good friends Oleg Filthirichski, the Russian aluminium-to-coffins magnate.

What Osborne failed to mention was that he was no stranger to the *Chernobyl II,* having on no fewer than five occasions rowed across in a dinghy in the middle of the night to implore our Russian friend to chip in a few million roubles to the Tory fighting fund.

Osborne even suggested that they could get round the law by paying the money through one of Mr Filthirichski's British companies, the Mayfair and Paddington Steam Laundering Service ("Make It Quick, Make It Clean!"), so that no one would suspect that something fishy was going on.

None of this need ever have come to light but for Osborne's failure to observe the golden rule – "What a chap says to another chap when he's at another chap's house should jolly well remain a secret between the chaps in question."

N. ROTHSCHILD, London

(Signed by P. Mandelson in Mr Rothschild's absence)

Isn't It Terrible The Way Politicians Are So Greedy For Money?

Asks Max Hastings

IT IS sickening to read yet again of our sleazy money-grubbing politicians buzzing around millionaires like flies on a dung heap. *(Note to editor: You did say three grand, didn't you? M.H.)*.

Can they not see how unattractive this behaviour appears to decent honest hard-working people like myself? *(Is this enough? M.H.) Not if you want your three grand. Ed.)*

I was talking to a banking friend while we were shooting last Wednesday and he said how pathetic it was that these politicians were so desperate to mix with rich people from the City. *(Will this do? M.H. No. Keep going. Ed.)*

Why can't they just do the job they are paid for instead of scrounging off rich people like my good friend Lord Rothermere?

© *Hastingstrashforcash 2008*

"Yes, but it's becoming more than an evening tipple isn't it, Nigel?"

THE PRINCESS AND THE PEANUTS

by Mother Goosestep

ONCE upon a time there was a pushy princess who lived in a lovely palace and paid peanuts in rent until, one day, the wicked Queen said, "Look, I've been subsidising you for years, but it really is time you coughed up."

Then the princess wept and wept and begged for mercy, saying, "I have no money and my husband cannot even afford a razor to shave off his silly beard."

But the wicked Queen was hard of heart and said, "If you don't like it, you can pushy off."

And the whole nation rejoiced and were happy ever after.

GLENDA SLAGG

Fleet Street's Favourite Dollygarch!

■ HATS OFF to fearless Fern Britton!?! She's the fun-loving fatso who is not ashamed to tell the world about her Gastric Band!?!! *(What's that? Ed.)* Hang on, I'm coming to that – it's stapling up your tummy to stop all the cake getting into your gut!?! *(Thanks. I always wanted to know. Ed.)* Anyway, as I was saying, *This Morning*'s once Ten-Ton Tessa is now Beanpole Bessie and it's all down to that lil' ol' Gastric Band!?! Can you hear them playing?! Is it "Food, Glorious Food" they are strummin'?! No sirree!? More like "Tea For None"!? Geddit?

■ FATTY FERN!?! What a disgrace!?! Pretendin' she's been a-slimmin' and a-trimmin' with just a few crumbs of Ryvita to keep her going through the gruellin' task of presenting *This Morning*!?! And all the time her dramatic weight loss was down to an elastic band twisted round her gut to stop the cake going down!? *(Alright. We've done this bit. Ed.)* Role model?! More like a Roly-Poly Pudding model!?! Do us all a favour, Fern!?!

And staple up your gob rather than your gut!?! Geddit?!

■ *WARNING, Mister!? Get your Kleenex out!?! Cos Billie Piper's just had a little 'un!?! All together!?! Aaah!?! And who's that a-droolin' and a-dribblin'?!? Not the tiny tot, stoopid, it's carrot-haired Chris Evans, Billie's creepy ex!?!! Take a tip from Aunty Glenda, Chris!?! Get in Prezza's car and join him in a one-way trip off Beachy Head!?! (Have you been drinking again? Ed.) OK, so I have – doesn't everyone at ten o'clock in the morning?! I've been out with troubled Kerry Katona!? What a gal!?! Who is she again? (You're fired. Ed.)*

■ HERE THEY ARE – Glenda's Halloween Rumpy-Pumpkins!?!
● **Oleg Deripaska.** Fancy a bit of olegover round at my place?!
● **Juande Ramos.** So you couldn't score and you got the sack?! Jump into my sack and score any time!?!
● **Benjamin Wegg-Prosser.** Crazy name, crazy guy!?!!!

Byeee!!

Dave Snooty AND HIS PALS

Alan Bennett Donates Literary Archive To The Bodleian Library

That Bequest In Full (annotated by the Author)

● **One tupperware box** – containing uneaten egg and cress sandwiches.

● **Half packet chocolate Hobnobs** – consumed by members of cast of "The Madness of Boy George" during rehearsal.

● **One pair bicycle clips** – originally purchased from gentlemen's outfitters Pevsner and Snelgrove in Halifax, now a hairdressers and nail bar with the unfortunate name of "Snips 'n' Clips". (The letters "a" and "d", I notice, having sadly been snipped and clipped from the word "and").

● **One letter to Thora Hird** – enquiring if she would mind playing the part of Mrs Hoover, an old lady who takes the No. 42 bus to visit her niece, who works behind the perfume counter at Boots in Giggleswick.

● **A "Good Luck" card to Dame Maggie Smith** – from the author when she took over the role of Mrs Hoover in "Forty Plays On" at the Gielgud in Shaftesbury Avenue. Bears the message, *"Wish You Were Hird"*, not a bad joke given the unfortunate circumstances.

● **An Order of Service from Evensong from the Church of St Melvyn in Bragg, Cumbria** – A note in pencil on the sheet by the author enquires whether or not the vicar, who has a prominent moustache, might indeed "bat and bowl for the same side".

(That's enough archive. Ed.)

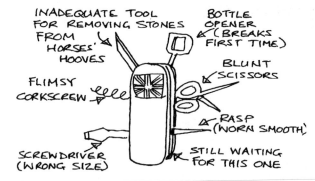

BRITISH ARMY KNIFE

- INADEQUATE TOOL FOR REMOVING STONES FROM HORSES' HOOVES
- BOTTLE OPENER (BREAKS FIRST TIME)
- BLUNT SCISSORS
- FLIMSY CORKSCREW
- RASP (WORN SMOOTH)
- SCREWDRIVER (WRONG SIZE)
- STILL WAITING FOR THIS ONE

EVENING STANDARD FRIDAY 31 OCTOBER

She's back! And she's bigger-headed than ever!

Mary Ann Bighead on the rise of Portfolio Woman

Many of you are probably wondering what I'm up to these days. Well the answer is, inevitably, more than you. Yes, I am now a Portfolio Woman combining successful motherhood – of Brainella, PHd, 7 and Intelligencia, MLitt, 3 – with what I call multi-faceted career streams (or "being freelance" if you're not as clever as me!).

I am an entrepreneur, broadcaster, writer, non-executive director, wife, parent and all-round big-head! How on earth did I do it? And can you? Well, it helps to be incredibly clever, so this may rule out quite a lot of you as you won't have been a city editor, columnist, TV pundit, travel writer and holder of the Croix de Grande Tête, 1st Class awarded by the French Government, but if you are brave, bold and of course brilliant a Portfolio Life can be yours.

Just one thing – don't hide your light under a bushel. Portfolio Woman has to be prepared to tell people how much cleverer she is than everyone else – or how would they know? Not everyone reads the Evening Standard!

So my advice is "Go For It" girl! – unless you are not very clever in which case "Forget It"! I'm writing this at home, by the way, on my laptop avoiding having to go anywhere and combining working with enjoying a wonderful lifestyle that you haven't got! Clever or what? (Answer: Even cleverer than you can imagine!)

© Mary Ann Bighead *The Evening Standard 2008*

What You Missed

The Today Programme

Radio 4

John Humphrys *(for it is he)*: And now, the government's plan to introduce compulsory sex lessons for the under-fives. In our Nuneaton studio we have the educational adviser to the Department for Children, Innovation and Lifelong Skills, Kevin Dimwit. Mr Dimwit, is this really what we want? Sex education in nursery schools?

Dimwit: Well you know we are rolling out a new classroom programme…

Humphrys: So, will the lessons contain words like "penis" and "condom"? Is that the sort of thing we want toddlers to hear and repeat to their parents when they get home?

Dimwit: Well, er, you know John, what we are looking at is an innovative attempt to introduce…

Humphrys: Words like "vagina" and "clitoris" and "anal penetration"? Is that what we're going to hear? Let's be frank about this, I mean the next thing we know people will be saying these things on the radio at 8.15 in the morning during the school run in order to spice up their dreary programmes. Isn't that what's going to happen? Condom? Arse? Fellatio?

Posh woman: And now, thought for the day with the editor of Playboy magazine, the Reverend Simon Heffner.

Heffner: You know, in a very real sense we all need sex education throughout our lives and who amongst us can honestly put his hand on his penis and say *(cont. p. 94)*

"Just 'Bong'? That's not much of a ringtone!"

A Taxi Driver writes

EVERY week a well-known taxi-driver is invited to go on a tour of America by the BBC. This week, **Stephen Fry**, Cab No. 0112358 (the opening digits of the Fibonacci Sequence, as it happens).

When one contemplates the vastness of the geophysical landscape, from the deserts of New Dworkin to the moist tufty swamps of deepest Obama, one's senses (nine, not five as is commonly supposed) are overwhelmed by mystery, wonder and awe at the sheer size, scale, silliness, solitude, serendipity, zippedydoodahzippedyday, flagwaving trumpet-blowing oompahpah Americanness of the whole ridiculous, wondrous scrumptiousness of... where am I again? I had that Simon Schama in the back of my cab. And Griff Rhys Jones. Bless!

"Can the media hype me up any more?"

"YES, WE CAN!"

The Birth Of The Messiah

by **Matthew, Mark, Luke and Jonathan Freedland**

AND LO it came to pass that an Angel of the Lord appeared on CNN and said, "Fear not for I bring you breaking tidings of great joy – for this day in the city of Washington a Messiah has come, and his name shall be Obama, which is to say 'the Chosen One, the Saviour, the Bringer of Change'."

And there were hacks sleeping it off in the fields and they saw the light and said one to another, "Truly this man is the Son of God. Let us go and worship Obama."

And the hacks went and anointed Obama, writing hundreds of pieces about him saying, "Verily, he is a dream cometh true."

And shortly it came to pass that the people cried out for miracles, saying, "Surely Superman has come amongst us. Why can he not fix the US economy, bring about global peace and feed us all with 5,000 quarter-pound cheeseburgers, shakes and fries?"

And Obama said unto

them, "Blessed are the Peacemakers, for they shall be redeployed from Iraq to take part in a new surge in Afghanistan."

And the people said amongst themselves, "Hang on, this doesn't seem all that different to that which goeth on before even under Dubya, the Burning Bush." *(Cont. Chapter 94.)*

Special 94-Page Obama Souvenir Pull-Out Supplement

★A Dream Comes True★

From herding goats with a baseball bat on a Hawaiian surfboard to sitting behind the Oval Office desk in the White House is an incredible journey. And the man who is taking that journey for us all is **Barack Hussein Obama**.

A NEW world dawns... We are all changed utterly... A giant leap for mankind... Earth has not anything to show more fair... Bliss was it in that dawn to be alive... Everyone will remember where they were... A nation united at last... He's got the whole world in his hands... I'd like to teach the world to sing... And I think to myself what a wonderful world... *(Continues for 94,000 words)*

ON OTHER PAGES

You Name The Obama Puppy

Choose from the following:

● Pluto   ● Sarko   ● Beyonce
● Dubya   ● Oprah   ● Peaches
● Hillary   ● Gordon   ● Stephen Fry

MEET THE CLINTSTONES – THE PREHISTORIC FIRST FAMILY

Yes! They are back yet again!

"Secretary of State? But don't I have to be abroad all the time?"

"That's the idea!!"

"Bill is going to be happy anyway!"

"I'm going to be in charge of Iraq and Afghanistan!"

"Obama's no fool is he! Still at least this time I won't..."

"...be sleeping with the Secretary!"

YABADABBADOBAMA!!!

GLENDA SLAGG
EXCLUSIVE!

She's the gal leading the backlash against the backlash!!?

■ LIGHTEN UP Manuel!?! *Que?!?* Andrew Sachs I'm talkin' about stoopid!?! What's the matter, Grandad? Can't you take a joke?!? Wossy and Wussy were just a pair of pranksters havin' a little laugh!?!! And you've turned it into a Third World War!?! Get a life – or what's left of it!?! Geddit?! There's only one thing Fawlty around here and that's *your* sense of humour!?! It's *you* who should have got the Sachs – not Russell!?!

■ MANUEL'S granddaughter!?! What a slapper!?! She deserves everything she got!!? Miss Innocent!?! Don't make me laugh!?! "Burlesque Entertainer"? Oh yeah! Come off it, darlin', and don't tell me you didn't enjoy your night of nookie with Randy Romeo Russell!?! Mmmmm!?! There's plenty of us gals who would happily have swapped places with you!??! It was only a phone call to your Granddad, luv, not the Third World War!?!

■ WHAT'S the matter with everyone?!? Have we all turned into prudes and killjoys overnight?!? I thought we got rid of Mrs Whitehouse and her ilk years ago!?! This country has always enjoyed raunchy humour – Chaucer, Shakespeare and now Risqué Russell and his own *Brand* of cutting edge, boundary-breaking abusive phone calls!?! So don't go, Russy and Rossy – in these dark times of recession we need you more than ever to keep us laughin' by ringing up old blokes and giving them grief about their granddaughter!?!

■HATS OFF to Ross and Russ!?! The Dirty Duo who have put Britain on top of the world – when it comes to dirty messages on pensioners' answerphones, these two comedy giants have made us hold our heads high!?! *(That's enough Backlash. Ed.)*

Byeee!!

THOSE BBC MEASURES IN THE WAKE OF 'SACHS-GATE" IN FULL

Alistair Haircut
The former senior marketing executive with Sky has been recruited to head a six strong "Stop Presenters Insulting Sitcom Pensioners By Saying They've F***ed Their Granddaughters" monitoring department, on a salary of £320,000 a year.

Toby Trendy
The former head of stolen formats at ITV has been recruited to head a twelve-strong "Monitoring The Monitoring Department Department" to monitor the effectiveness of the internal monitoring. Toby will report directly to Alistair Haircut on a salary of £285,000 a year.

Bruce Juice
The former Head of Paperclips at Channel 5 will have a floating role, both monitoring the monitor's monitoring and monitoring what monitoring of broadcasts needs monitoring on a salary of £275,000 a year.

Brian de Rivative
The former head of mergers and acquisitions at Lehman Brothers will head a twelve-strong team developing an internal framework to allow the establishment of numerous internal monitoring departments to monitor the internal monitoring departments on a salary of £567,000 a year.

James Beancounter
The former head of Jam Sponges with Unilever will report directly to the Director General about how many fresh layers of bureaucracy will be required to stop Jonathan Ross ringing up Andrew Sachs to tell him that Russell Brand "f***ed his granddaughter" on a salary of £800,000 a year.

"We were only pushing the boundaries, Your Honour. It is part of our cultural remit"

"As a stand-up comic, I feel that I'm a lightning conductor for society...

... I say the unsayable, I'm transgressive, for me there are no taboos...

... Criticise Jonathan Ross and Russell Brand?! Me? You're joking!"

ME AND MY SPOON

THIS WEEK

JONATHAN ROSS

Do you have a favourite spoon?

Yes. Look at this one. What does it remind you of? That's right. A bloke's knob. A great big pork sausage looking for some stuffing! Though it's not as big as mine. Let me show you! Come on, darling, you're gagging for it, aren't you? I'll give you a good spooning...

(Unfortunately, due to a number of complaints from our readers, we have decided to suspend this column for three months. However, we must stress that we reserve our right as a public service magazine to publish cutting-edge spoon interviews that push back the boundaries of acceptable cutlery feature pieces at some future date. The Board of Private Eye Trustees. 2008.)

Lives of the Saints and Martyrs No. 94

St Charles of Moore

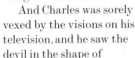

AND IN those times there was a holy man, a scribe named Charles, who shunned the wickedness of the world and shut himself away in a rustic cell to write about the life and miracles of the Blessed Margaret of Thatcher.

And Charles was sorely vexed by the visions on his television, and he saw the devil in the shape of Jonathan Ross. And Charles waxed wroth that he should have to pay to witness these blasphemies.

So he declared to the authorities that he would render no tribute to the BBC, but would rather be chained, bound and incarcerated for his beliefs.

And there were many simple folk who followed his example, saying that they too did not want to pay up.

But the BBC took no notice, thinking that Charles would eventually go away and everyone would forget all about him.

And they were not wrong.

'BLAIR WAS ALWAYS A CONSERVATIVE,' Top Aide Claims

by Our Religious Correspondent **Christina O'Fatherlhavesinned**

ONE OF Tony Blair's former top lieutenants last night revealed that during his years in Downing Street, Tony Blair had been "a secret Conservative all along".

The former Prime Minister told viewers to the popular religious programme *Good Morning Has Broken*, "It is true that I have always been strongly drawn towards Conservatism, which is a strong and ancient faith. I have long been attracted to the example of the Blessed Margaret Thatcher, but I could never admit this openly when I was in power. People would have thought that I was a bit of a nutter and I could have lost my job.

"But," Mr Blair continued, "I now feel free to talk openly about my faith and my beliefs, which is why I now go every morning to the bank to worship money.

Holy In The Wall

"My wife has always been a devout capitalist and was always trying to get me to make as much money as I could. And now at last I am free to do so without any pretence."

During his 10 years at Number Ten, Tony Blair played down his Conservative convictions, telling journalists "I don't do greed".

But now he is no longer ashamed to profess his true Conservative beliefs to all the world.

"Sometimes I feel like everyone's trying to wind me up"

THOSE TEN POLICE PLEDGES IN FULL

1 If you ring 999 we pledge that your call may be monitored for training purposes.

2 When ringing 999 you should press 1 for physical assault, 2 for rape, 3 to pay a parking fine, 4 to hear the options again. We pledge to answer ALL your calls within two working days.

3 If you have been the victim of a serious crime such as burglary and are upset about it, we pledge to send round a counsellor to talk through your traumatic experience (subject to availability).

4 If you have been the victim of a serious crime such as burglary and are NOT upset about it, we pledge to arrange a visit from a community support officer to talk through your lack of trauma at a time suitable to you (11.30am Thursday morning).

5 We pledge to make a number of further pledges involving the words community, neighbourhood, social fabric, grapefruit segments, etc.

6 If you are a Brazilian electrician innocently boarding an underground train we pledge to fire at least 15 bullets into your head without warning and then tell a lot of lies at the inquest.

7 If you are Sir Ian Blair, we pledge to pay you £400,000 for being fired. (That's enough pledges. Ed)

It's time for this self-important idiot to put a sock in it

Writes Sir Max Hastings (Journalist of the Year 1971)

SCARCELY A day goes by without the future king of England giving us his views on pretty well every subject under the sun.

We hear him droning on about GM crops, alternative medicine, the Prayer Book, windfarms and modern architecture.

Why should we listen to a man who clearly knows nothing about any of the subjects he is sounding off about, and who is obviously just making it up as he goes along.
(Is this enough yet? – MH).
(No, another 800 words please – PD).

Anyone would think that rather than being heir to the throne he was actually a highly paid newspaper columnist.
(Will this do? – MH).
(No. You're fired – PD).

21

ROMANTIC SHORT STORY SPECIAL

'Life Begins At...'

by DAME SYLVIE KRIN, best-selling author of *Heir Of Sorrows*

THE STORY SO FAR:
Charles is 60 and Camilla has prepared a surprise party at Highgrove.

Now read on...

THE SOUND of champagne corks popping mingled with the excited laughter of the guests, as Charles looked on delightedly at the glittering array of celebrities cavorting before him on the dance floor to the sound of Bonzo Bilk and his Billericay Banjo Band.

"Ying Tong Ying Tong Ying Tong Tiddle Eye Po," Charles hummed along merrily to himself.

"They don't write songs like that any more, do they, darling?" he beamed at Camilla as they foxtrotted around the floor.

And who was this they had just brushed up against? Sir Stephen Fry dancing with the newly ennobled Lord Mandelson. And wasn't that the Indian chap from the Kumars, jitterbugging with Lady Euphorbia Lycett-Green? And was that Eddie Fox stepping lightly on Dame Jilly Cooper's toes? Had he ever been happier? His nearest and dearest all celebrating this historic day together.

His thoughts were interrupted momentarily by the roar of a Chinook helicopter landing in the Islamic Garden.

"That must be Wills and Harry," he cried excitedly.

"They remembered!" And indeed they had. The two young princes in fancy dress as members of the Wehrmacht stumbled onto the dance floor, along with their friends Pongo Fforbes-Frobisher, Charlie Ricketson-Smythe, Fruitella Chelsea-Tractor, Pussina Wellington-Bosanquet and a number of people they had met in Boozo's Nightclub in Kensington shortly before.

"What ho, Pater! Great thrash! Where's the booze?" shouted the second-in-line to the throne.

Charles smiled paternally. "There's some organic elderflower cordial in the marquee, I think. Sir Alan knows where it is."

"Ha, ha, ha, jokes," laughed the young people, as they staggered towards the Champagne Bar where Sir Alan Fitztightly was dispensing flutes of Duchy Original Poundbury Champagne-style Drink to Sir Ben Elton and Sir Rowan Atkinson, amongst others.

But then Camilla was clapping her hands and calling for silence.

"Good evening, everybody, and thank you so much for coming all this way. And now for tonight's big surprise."

For a second, the thought flashed through Charles' mind. Was Mater abdicating? Did Camilla know something he didn't? It would be quite a birthday present.

But no. The grey-bearded drummer of the Billericay Banjo Band, the legendary Ronnie Gibbons, performed a roll on the drums and Camilla continued, "Please welcome our special guest, the one and only er... Rob Stewart, is it?"

And into the spotlight strode the tousled and tanned popmeister, the man of a

hundred hits and a thousand conquests, dressed in leopard-skin trousers with a guitar strung around his neck.

"Yeah. Happy Birthday, Yer Highness. This one's for you," drawled Rod Stewart in his familiar husky voice.

And then he launched into his most famous chartbuster, as the guests swayed and sang along. "Do ya think I'm Sixty," they all chanted raucously...

"WHAT A great party! He really is incredible for his age, isn't he?"

Charles' ears pricked up, as he stood in the queue for the buffet serving vegetarian Lobster Thermidor with Free-Trade Hand-Reared Swan, and could not help himself overhearing a conversation between two of his younger guests standing in front of him, Lady Araminta "Minty"

Starborgling and her friend Tara Rara-Boomdeeay.

"He's like *so* not past it. you'd never know he was that old. He's like really fit still," observed Minty.

Charles felt a warm glow rising from the pit of his stomach.

Young people were often misjudged, he felt. They were actually very perceptive and really saw things the way they were.

"A lot of people say like he's finished and that," added Tara, "but I say he's still sexy and he's like sort of good for years and years."

How true that was, Charles told himself, and how heartening at a time when the ghastly chaps in the press were so relentlessly negative and so unnecessarily critical. Here was the authentic voice of tomorrow.

"He's had a hard life, right, and his first wife was a nightmare..." continued Lady Araminta.

Charles nodded silently as he helped himself to a vegan poppadum with grilled kiwi fruit and baked beansprout sauce.

Minty then turned to Charles, "Don't you agree, sir? I mean, Rod Stewart's amazing, isn't he?"

"Er... er... Yes, I suppose he is," Charles stammered dejectedly.

He looked down at his plate and felt his appetite rapidly dwindle away. The Billericay Banjo Band struck up once again with *I'm Walking Backwards To Christmas.*

To be continued...)

THAT BNP LIST IN FULL

The shocking names the press is too scared to publish

KNACKER, Inspector PFI. 999 Acacia Avenue, London SW19.
Occupation Senior member of Thames Regional Porn Squad.
Recreations Judo, small arms and engaging in Masonic rituals with other members of the force.

GUSSETT, Reginald. The Berghof, Berchtesgaden Suburb, Beds.
Occupation Archivist and local historian, publications include *Highways and Byways of Victorian Bedfordshire* and *Why Enoch Was Right*.
Recreations Researching the Gussett family tree and English representative of the Klu Klux Klan.

PUGG, Dave. 106a Churchill Drive, Billericay, Essex.
Occupation Night club bouncer.
Recreations Supporting Millwall FC and Secretary of The Den "Keep Racism In Football" Campaign.

VAN HOOGSTRATEN, Major Vernon. The Bursary, St Cake's School, Solihill, W. Midlands.
Occupation School bursar and head of rifle shooting at well-known West Midlands independent public school (Motto: Strength through joy).
Recreations Weightlifting and researching the history of torture.

SNOZZER, Ronnie. 17 Mosley Crescent, London E17.
Occupation Black cab driver (the cab, not Mr Snozzer!). Gatwick £40. Phone 071974 351351.
Recreations Phoning Talk Radio to agree with views of Mr John Gaunt on all subjects and "dogging".

WILMOT, Dawn. Flat C, 117 The Franco Estate, Mussolini Road, Streatham.
Occupation Proprietor of hairdressing saloon "Hair Hitler" in Peckham High Street.

Recreations Giving "Third Reiki Massage" and microwave cooking.

ROUGH TROUSER, Rev Oliver. The Order of Sodomites Retirement Home, Bury St. Edmunds, Suffolk.
Occupation Retired Clerk-in-holy-orders.
Recreations Mediaeval vestments and the young male nude in art history.
(That's enough Fascists, Ed)

GRIFFIN LASHES OUT AT BNP LIST SHOCK

OBERSTURMFUEHRER Nick "Goebbels" Griffin, leader of the British National Party, today welcomed the publication of the list, saying that it showed how the media stereotype of BNP members as "goose-stepping, jack-booted, swivel-eyed lunatics" was completely wrong.

"As the list demonstrates," he said, "the BNP membership is made up of a thoroughly respectable cross-section of decent British goose-stepping, jack-booted, swivel-eyed lunatics."

"Darling, you didn't tell me you were a member of the BNP"

The Eye says
Baby P – A Scene From Hell

THE story of Baby P is one which has rightly shocked the nation to its core. The details of the short and tragic life of the this innocent toddler are so shocking and so depraved that few readers could possibly want to dwell on them in any detail. That is why we have decided to devote 48 pages to this horrifying story every day this week.

PLUS: Baby P – The Pictures That Are Too Shocking To Print, pages 48-96.

The Sun Says
Baby P – A Scene From Hell

THE tragic and shocking case of Baby P has revealed to a horrified nation what sickening abuse can be meted out by cruel, sadistic bullies.

So, it's only right that in response to this we demand that all the social workers, council officials and doctors involved in the case are named, shamed and then beaten to death. *(Is this right? Ed.)*

Damning Childcare Report Into Damning Childcare Reports

by Our Social Work Correspondent **Phil Formzin**

A DAMNING childcare report was released today damning a damning childcare report released two days ago.

This damning report highlights systemic failures in the way the damning childcare report damned a previous damning childcare report into damning allegations that the damning childcare reports weren't sufficiently damning.

Ministers said that in the wake of this latest damning childcare report into the systemic failure of damning childcare reports a damning childcare report into this latest damning childcare report would be *(cont. for 94 years)*

DIARY

NIGELLA'S CHRISTMAS TURKEY

I always say that there's nothing quite so voluptuous as a Christmas Turkey. When I see it there, all bronzed and sizzling on our dining table, its legs akimbo, its plump breasts so vast, so juicy, so succulent, so beseeching – yes, in that instant I know the meaning of *l'amour*.

We all have our own ways of handling the seductive charms of the moist turkey. Some probe; others delve. Some dive deep, deep, deep, while others prefer to give all their attention to the skin, imbibing that gorgeous scent through whatever orifices come to hand then licking, tearing, gobbling and – oh yes! – swallowing.

Turkey is, to my mind, best consumed within the softly enfolding after-glow of a full moon. Oh, to nibble on the most slender sliver of breast as the silver-blue light shimmers enticingly upon its juicy curves! Then, and only then, can one fully experience the taste-bud heaven that is turkey.

Ingredients: One 12lb turkey; 900g good sausage meat.

Your fresh young turkey will come trussed and bound, naked but for great swathes of string tightly bound around its chest and its legs and its *derrière*. "I am your obedient slave!" it seems to be saying, "Do with me what you will!"

But all naughty turkeys must learn their lesson. Ignore its beseechings. This is the time to leave it just as it is, unable to move, while you go off and enjoy yourself. Why not pour yourself a delicious warm bath, full of the most exotic oils and unguents? Return to the kitchen in your own good time and you will find the turkey still there, still trussed up and rigid, its body almost quivering in anticipation of what you are about to do to it.

You've had your fun. Now is the time to act! With a few deft strokes, slide your fingers all over its body, removing every last bit of string or trussing from your turkey and thus shake it free of all bondage. Immediately, it will seem to expand. Now go deep within and wash the inside of your bird with ice-cold running-water. Never mind the drips! How glamorous it now looks, and how liberated! The sight of the washed turkey, it always reminds me of Anita Ekberg dancing in the Trevi fountain in La Dolce Vita. Call me silly, but for some reason, I've always had this thing about water glistening on the bare shoulders of a naked turkey.

Drain well, and blot dry with kitchen towels, taking care to pamper those hidden crevices. I've always loved to guide my fingers delicately through all those long-lost nooks and crannies, playing my beloved turkey like a grand piano. Sometimes, I will invite friends over for a turkey-blotting party. One by one, we all take it in turns to smother the bounteous bird with all the love we can muster.

Pre-heat the oven to 200° C/gas 6.

Take your turkey and, using your finger tips, *pry*. Wiggle some space between the skin and those vast, accommodating breasts. Into this space, squeeze your sausage meat, pushing, pressing, coaxing and surging so that it covers the whole breast, in all its magnificent glory. Some people prefer to use oil all over, just to give it that faint but undeniable frisson that always comes when fingers touch skin. Others like to dress it in something fabulous from Vivienne Westwood. *Chacun a son gout*, as they say in La France. Now, from on top of the skin, mould it with your outstretched hand so that the breast is voluptuously but smoothly bulging. By now it should be yielding to your every touch, and begging you silently for more.

Secure the flaps of skin over the oozing cavity with a meat skewer so that the sausage meat doesn't escape during the roasting. If, despite all your warnings, it does manage to escape then you will be left with no alternative but to whack it back in with a resounding thump. Another skewer may well be in order, methinks! Ouch! Be sure to let that little turkey minx know who's boss!

Now squeeze your turkey breast securely into a skin-tight tin and let it roast for about 2 hours and 40 minutes, basting periodically. An excellent idea for a get-together with friends and family is to throw a basting party, where between ten (10) and twenty (20) guests take turns to open the oven door and, clutching tight to your most curvaceous and voluminous ladle, to pour those fragrant juices all over the outstretched bird, thus keeping it wonderfully juicy and moist. Baste! Baste! Baste! More! Yes! Yes! YES!

When you think it's ready, press and – yes! – pierce your turkey with your long blade, preferably around that luscious area where the leg meets the rest of the body. Take it slowly, very slowly. Just lie back and wait, letting those precious juices trickle out. Lick! Lick! Lick! Mmmm!

After it's all over, why not pull a cracker or two – or better still, get a close friend or two to pull them with you? Mmmmm!

As told to CRAIG BROWN

Letter to the Editor
Names of the year

From the Rev. A. Cyclone-Nargis.

Sir, As usual at this time of year, I have compiled a list of the most popular names of 2008, as recorded in your Birth's column. They are as follows:

Boys	Girls
1. Barack	Carla
2. Libor	Hillary
3. Gaza	Australia
4. Fabio	Mammamia
5. Boris	Fern
6. Mosley	Britney
7. Trig	Cheryl
8. Ross	Keira
9. Russell	Deripaska
10. Baby P.	Baroness
Worsthorne	Scotland

THE REV. A. CYCLONE-NARGIS, The Old Storm Shelter, 1 Burma Road, Mandalay, Beds.

GORDON'S DAY OF SHAME

by Our News of the World Staff **Phil Wallet**

CELEBRITY PM Gordon Brown has been caught being unfaithful to his long-time partner, Prudence.

The Prime Minister has begun a not-very-secret relationship with a notorious boom and busty blonde called Plenty O'Money, a former consort of the Conservative Party.

Despite years of pretending to be a loyal and upright family savings man, with his four-letter catchphrase "Fife", Gordon now stands revealed as a profligate, two-timing, reckless, shameless, spendthrift

(cont. p. 94)

That Gordon Ramsay 'Slapper-Up' Menu in Full

Welsh Rarebit on the Side

– ✳ –

Legover of Pork

– ✳ –

Crispy Fuck on a Bed of Cheap Hotel

– ✳ –

Spotted Dick

(by News of the World)

– ✳ –

To drink: *Plonker*

(That's enough menu, Ed.)

You too can make Gordon's Xmas Recipe for Disaster by logging on to Gordon@howaboutaquickFWord.co.fuk

POLLY FILLER
on the Mama Mia Phenomenon

NORMALLY, it's just the sort of thing I hate. Soft-centred, sentimental, escapist, and worst of all, a musical! Added to which, I have always hated Abba, Meryl Streep leaves me cold, Piers Brosnan gives me the creeps and Colin Firth makes me want to shout at the screen.

But as soon as I put on the DVD (and my partner, the Useless Simon, walked out to watch Boris Johnson on Top Gear on Dave Gold 2 Plus One in the kitchen), I knew that Mamma Mia was the best film in the history of the cinema.

Why? It's big-hearted, emotional and a world away from the boring grind of everyday life. And it's got great music by the Swedish pop legends Abba. Not to mention a wonderfully warm performance by Meryl Streep, the dishy Piers Brosnan giving me goosebumps and Colin Firth who makes me want to scream at the screen with laughter!

BUT YOU know what really made me like Mamma Mia?

The fact that everybody else does! I'm certainly not going to sit here looking like a sour-faced old killjoy whilst Rachel Johnson and Jenni Murray, and even Jeanette Winterson, for God's sake, are getting their faces in the paper saying how great it is! If every other female journalist of a certain age is jumping on the bandwagon, Polly Filler is not going to be left out!

No way, Fernando! So let's hear it for Mamma Mia!

And if they are looking for a Polly Filler quote for the DVD case, how about *"It's Mamma Mania! This show is Abba-solutely Fabba-ulous! Now gimme gimme gimme my money money money before midnight!"*
© All newspapers.

"I'm not too happy about the au pair trying to send gas home to Bulgaria"

Telegraph Xmas Charity Appeal 2008
Phone-In Day

This Christmas, times are tougher than ever and a lot of people are feeling the pinch – largely because we've sacked them.

So, this Sunday we're asking you to ring up some of the Telegraph's best-known names to whom we've given the boot and pledge them some money. Please help make their Christmas a happy one – unlike us. Even a small amount can go some way to make up for the fact that they're fired.

Thank you.

Thirsty Will Lewis, Editor

POETRY CORNER

In Memoriam Harold Pinter O.M., dramatist

So. Farewell
Then Harold Pinter,
Famous playwright.

The Birthday Party,
The Homecoming,
No Man's Land –
These were your
Masterpieces.

But now you have
Gone to
No man's land.

There will be
No more birthday parties

And no
Homecoming.

E.J. Thribb (17½)

The Pinter I knew

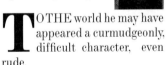

by Everybody

TO THE world he may have appeared a curmudgeonly, difficult character, even rude.

Yet to those of us who knew him well Harold was the most delightful of companions, charming, witty, generous to a fault, and with an impish sense of humour.

I well remember one magical evening at his favourite restaurant, Les Trois Etoiles de Michelin, when he was introduced to my young niece, who had just returned from a holiday in America.

Harold turned to her and in his inimitable way told her to "Fuck off back to fucking America with all your warmongering Fascist friends".

His other great love was cricket, and I shall never forget *(cont. p.94.)*

25

'I Am Not To Blame,' Say All Those To Blame

by Our Entire Parliamentary Staff

A WEEPING Speaker Martin openly admitted that he was in no way to blame for having allowed the police to storm Parliament and arrest an MP.

"It is true," he said, bringing out several onions simultaneously, "that I was told about this outrage in advance, but it is not my job to decide who is allowed to storm Parliament and arrest MPs. That is the job of that silly woman Mrs Pay, who was foolish enough to accept the job of Serjeant-at-Arms when I offered it to her, even though she knew she was a token woman who was only brought in on my advice to annoy the Queen."

Fighting back his tears, the Speaker continued, "I am not to blame for the fact that the police did not even have a warrant before forcing their way into the House of Commons. I can hardly be expected to ask every policeman who wants to storm Parliament whether they have some piece of paper or other to authorise them to do so.

"As I said earlier, that is the job of the silly woman with the horrible purple hair, who insisted, entirely against my better judgement, on accepting the job I gave her.

"Most of all," concluded the Speaker, "I am not to blame for being completely useless at my job. That is entirely the fault of New Labour and the snobbish public schoolboy Tony Blair who wanted a chippy, working-class Glaswegian toady in the chair to make it look as if Labour was still a working class party. And a fat lot of good it's done them all. Boo hoo hoo."

'I Am Not To Blame,' Says Top Policeman

ASSISTANT Chief Commissioner Sir Paul Stephenson angrily denied last night that he was in any way to blame for the appalling blunder he had made in ordering his men to storm Parliament without a warrant and arrest an MP.

"It is not my job," he said, "to check whether we have a warrant or not before we break into other people's premises. I leave that to my subordinates, like that ghastly little man, Bob Quick, who thinks he can beat me to the job of Britain's top policeman.

"And, anyway," Sir Paul continued, "if anyone is to blame for this fiasco, it is Boris Johnson, the London Mayor, for his interference in what is an operational police matter.

"Mr Johnson should have known that this matter was entirely my responsibility, except, of course, that it wasn't."

'Cripes! I Am Not To Blame,' Says Boris

A FURIOUS Mayor of London, Mr Boris Johnson, last night dismissed any suggestion that he was in any way to blame for the police operation against his friend Tory MP Damian Green.

"It would be entirely improper," said the Mayor, "for me to prejudge the police investigation into my friend's affairs, though it's pretty bloody obvious that the whole thing was a complete cock-up from start to finish, and a put-up job by Gordon and his boys to discredit Bojo and his mates in Parliament.

"If you ask me, I blame that ghastly woman, Jacqui Smith, but don't quote me."

'I Am Not To Blame,' Says Jacqui Smith

AN incandescent Home Secretary last night lashed out at critics who claimed that she was to blame for the entire Greengate crisis.

"It is not my job as Minister in Charge of the Police," said Ms Smith, "to supervise what the police get up to.

"It is true that I was quite rightly kept informed at every stage of what was going on, but I had no idea that the police were planning anything like this.

"If anyone is to blame for this fiasco, it is the Prime Minister, Gordon Brown, for appointing me to this job, when he knew perfectly well that I was in no way up to it."

'I Am Not To Blame,' Says PM

A SMILING Gordon Brown last night denied that the so-called Greengate affair could in any way be pinned on himself.

"I am not to blame," he said. "It is all the fault of that incompetent booby, the Speaker, in whom I have complete confidence and *(continued at top of this page)*

Mail Comment On The Speaker

Quentin Letts writes: Ha ha ha ha ha ha ha ha ha ha ha.

BLACK ROD

The Ancient Ceremony In Full

Black Rod: Knock, knock!

Speaker: Who's there?

Black Rod: The Police.

Speaker: Do come in and arrest anyone you want.

Serjeant-at-Arms: Oyez, Oyez!

"Do you mind? This is a quiet coach!"

POETRY CORNER
SPECIAL

In Memoriam Sir John Mortimer QC

So. Farewell
Then
John Mortimer

Author, Playwright,
Barrister and
Bon viveur.

You were most
Famous as the creator of
Rumpole of the
Bailey,

A poetry-loving barrister
Just like
Yourself.

Now you must
Go before
The greatest judge
Of all.

He who must
Be obeyed.

I hope you
Have prepared your
Case
And that he
Likes your books.

Then you
Will get off.

E.J. Thribb (17½)

In Memoriam Patrick McGoohan

So. Farewell
Then Patrick
McGoohan.

You were famous as
Number Six in
The Prisoner.

"Be seeing you" –
That was your
Catchphrase.

But we won't
Any more.

Who is Number One?

You probably
Have that information
Now that you
Really are
A free man.

E. J. Thribb (aka 17½
readers who sent this in)

In Memoriam David Vine, TV Presenter

So. Farewell
Then David
Vine, BBC
Sports commentator.

You will be remembered
For *Question Of Sport.*

"What happens
Next?" You used
To ask.

It is a question
We would now
Like to ask you.

E.J. Thribb (17½)

In Memoriam Tony Hart, Artist and Broadcaster

So. Farewell
Then Tony
Hart.

So many people
Have died
This week that
It is very
Difficult to think
Of anything else
To say.

Keith suggests
That it is
All too
Hart-breaking.

E.J. Thribb (17½)

Lines On The Departure From Office Of President George W. Bush

So. Farewell
Then George W. Bush,
Forty-third President of
The USA.

We never did discover
What the "W"
Stood for.

Keith says it was
"Warmonger".

Keith does say
Some very silly things
At times.

Eric J. Thribb (17½)

*F*IRST *D*RAFTS

Samuel Richardson

Thomas Hardy

Philip Roth

Arthur Ransome

THAT DE MENEZES CORONER'S SUMMING UP IN FULL

Ladies and gentlemen of the jury,

You have been sitting for some weeks with only one thing in mind. That you should be able to pronounce judgement on the conduct of the Metropolitan Police Force, namely Officers P, B and W, Superintendent Q and Chief Inspector Z. But it is my duty to advise you that, as the law stands, it is not in your remit to have any view of the matter whatsoever. You must strike it from your mind, as if you had never been present in this court.

You have heard several different accounts of these tragic events from a variety of witnesses, all of whom agree that the police opened fire on Mr Menezes with no warning, despite having no idea who he was. You have also witnessed the distressing sight of the deceased's mother, a foreign lady whom you might easily mistake for an illegal immigrant, who, being foreign and emotional, has been unable to control her feelings on a number of occasions, as we heard various policemen describing how they murdered her innocent son at the railway station in question. You are also to put this poor, unbalanced woman from your mind, as you reach the verdict which I shall now instruct you to give.

Your options, ladies and gentlemen, under the principle *custodes nunquam culpabilis*, are as follows. If you think that the police fired 15 bullets into Mr Menezes's head entirely in good faith, which was understandable, you may think, given the state of terrorist anarchy prevailing in the capital at the time, then you may deliver a verdict of "unfortunate killing".

If, on the other hand, you believe that the police made an entirely innocent mistake, and killed someone who might easily have been Osama bin Laden's right-hand man, judging by the suspicious way in which he was walking along, sending text messages on a mobile phone device before descending the escalator to board an underground train, then you must pronounce a verdict of "death by misadventure".

You may, alternatively, wish to commend the officers, whose evidence you have heard in this court, for the unfailing honesty of their testimony and their unflinching courage in standing up to the unwarranted attacks on their integrity made by various irresponsible members of the public – in this case, men and women who merely happened to be in the same railway carriage at the time, and whose memories of what they saw and heard may well be faulty, you may think, after the lapse of so much time.

And you will remember the moving sight of the brave, upright officer K9 who wept openly in the witness box, as he recalled how he warned the suspect repeatedly that he was a policeman and asked him to lay down his guns before reluctantly discharging his weapon into his head.

I must emphasise that the one verdict which you are not allowed to give is that of "unlawful killing by the police". Were you to be reckless enough to do so, you would each be charged with the very serious crime of delivering an unlawful verdict, which carries a maximum penalty of death, and I would have no choice but to sentence you to be taken from this place to an underground station and there to be shot by highly-trained police marksmen until you are dead.

It's Your Line To Red Ken On LBC

Ken: Next caller, please.

Caller: Hello, Ken, this is Colin from Colindale.

Ken: Hello, Colin.

Colin: As a lifelong left wing activist Ken, you must be appalled at the coroner's verdict in the Menezes case. I mean, the point is, Ken, the police have been given total license to shoot whoever they want. Isn't that right, Ken?

Ken: No, caller, I think you'll find that Sir Ian Blair and his officers acted in the best interest of Londoners and don't forget that, as Sir Ian pointed out, this was a fog of war situation and there are always unfortunately casualties in…

Colin: I don't believe I'm hearing this, Ken. What a load of boll…

Ken: Next caller, please.

Caller: Hi, Ken. This is Chelsey from Chelsea

Ken: Hello, Chelsey, you're through to Red Ken.

Caller: I mean, you know it's really scandalous – this Cressida Dick woman is still in the police and has even been promoted – don't you agree, Ken?

Ken: I absolutely do agree, Chelsey. If anyone deserves promotion it is Cressida, a fine officer as are all the outstanding police officers in London who are out on the streets risking their lives shooting unarmed civilians. Next caller, please.

Caller: It's Inspector Knacker here. Knacker of the Yard.

Ken: Hello, Inspector. I hope you are not calling me up to ask me about the finances of London when I was mayor or the unfortunate business of Mr Jasper and…

Knacker: No, Ken. Me and the boys just wanted to say love the programme and Happy Christmas to you and your listeners.

Ken: Thank you, Inspector. So, we have heard it from the horse's mouth. Boris to blame for the Stockwell shooting *(cont. 94 kHz)*

"I'm sorry, Watson, but with all this paperwork and targets to meet, I can't possibly take on another case"

BANKER'S $50 BILLION SCAM SHOCKS WORLD

by Our City Staff **Phil Boots**

MONEY men across the world were in a state of shock last night at the news that one of the world's top bankers had pulled off the greatest fraud in history.

Bernard Madoffwiththecash had swindled investors out of $50 billion in the most daring pyramid selling scheme since the time of the ancient pharaohs.

"It is absolutely outrageous," said one leading City investment banker, Fred Needle, "I mean, everyone knows that we bankers are all terrific crooks. But this is ridiculous – I mean, $50 billion is more than the rest of us have stolen all put together."

Through Hedge Fund Backwards

"And, to make matters worse, this crook has stolen the cash from his fellow crooks. Has the man no morals at all?

"Honestly, a lot of us are seriously out of pocket. I invested a lot of my clients' money in this obviously fraudulent scam, expecting to make millions myself, and what happens? The money vanishes into thin air. You've got to hand it to Mr Ripoff. Bloody brilliant. I wish I'd thought of it."

SUPERWOMAN INVESTS IN MADOFF

I've made a complete Horlicks of this

RESPECTED FINANCIAL GURU WAS FRAUDSTER SHOCK

by Our Wall Street Staff **Bernard Madoffwiththemoney**

A DISTINGUISHED senior figure in the world of banking was revealed last night to be "nothing more than a conman".

"Everyone in the City trusted him," said one financial commentator, "and investors put their faith in his ability to look after their savings."

Investment Bonkers

"In reality he just took their hard earned cash up front and then pretended to give it back to them by borrowing even more money."

Millions of ordinary people have lost everything and the fraudster himself confessed yesterday, "It was basically a giant *Gordonzi* scheme, just a form of pyramid selling in which the gullible public believed I have amazing financial acumen."

Gordon Brown continued, "The fact is that I've lost billions and billions of *(contd p 94)*.

The Madoff Victims

Otis B. Driftwood – CEO Driftwood Investments.

Herman Hackensacker III – Secretary, Palm Springs Golf Club.

The Royal Bank of Scotland.

Mrs Marty Schmuck – Director, Schmuck & Schmuck.

Irving P. Born-Yesterday Jnr – Chairman Born Yesterday Real Estate Co (Wyoming).

Howard – The bloke with glasses from the Halifax Ad.

El Stupido Banca di Espagna.

Rufus T. Firefly – Fund Manager, Firefly, Benson and Hedge Funds.

Save The Ant – Registered Charity (Antigua).

(That's enough greedy idiots. Ed)

"We were hijacked a week ago and I've only just found out"

Let's Parlez Franglais!

avec Le Late Kilometres Kington

Numero 94 Dans Le Maternity Ward

Docteur: Beaucoup de congratulations, Madame Dati! C'est une fille!

Rachida Dati (*pour c'est elle*): Taxi!

Docteur: Mais hangez-vous-on! Ou êtes-vous going?

Dati: Back à travail. Tout de suite. If not plus soon.

Docteur: Mais n'avons pas coupez le cord umbilical yet!

Dati: Il n'y a pas de temps for all cette nonsense. Je suis très modern et feminist et also un Minister important dans le gouvernment de Nicolas "Sexy" Sarkozy!

Docteur: Ah! Maintenant je comprends. Nurse! Bringez les high heels et le leopardskin jacket et le hairdryer et le make-up.

Dati: Au revoir Docteur!

Docteur: Un more chose, Madame! Je dois completer le birth certificate pour le petit bébé. Qui est le father?

Dati: Mindez votre own business!

Docteur: Zut alors! C'est David Blunkett, n'est-ce pas, le famous politician Anglais?

(Exit Madame Fruti pour spender some quality time avec les photographers)

29

'NEW YEAR FIREWORKS BIG SUCCESS,' SAY ORGANISERS

Dateline: 31st December

THIS YEAR's spectacular display of pyrotechnics which welcomed in the New Year over Gaza was "the best yet", said organisers.

Thousands came out of their houses in order to run away from the multi-million pound extravaganza put on for the benefit of Israeli voters *(Surely "Palestinians?" Ed.)*.

As phosphorous smoke lit up the night sky, there was general agreement that this year's display was the best since last year's and the one before that.

"It is something the Israelis do awfully well," said one bystander, Siddi Al-Bonkers. "Just look! Oooh! Aaaargh!"

MIDDLE EAST CRISIS

'WHERE IS BLAIR?'

asks nobody

by Our Man In Gaza **Chris Gunnfire**

AS THE crisis in the Middle East escalated yesterday, one question was on nobody's lips. Where is the man who was going to bring peace to that troubled region through his intensive round of non-stop after dinner speeches in China, former prime minister Tony Blair?

Said one Palestinian spokesman, speaking from his pile of rubble, "We deeply appreciate all the work Tony is doing for his bank in New York, but we wonder whether he could spare just a couple of minutes *(cont. p. 94.)*

NATIONWIDE OUTRAGE AT NEW YEAR ATROCITY

by Our Diplomatic Correspondent **Phil Pages**

NO ONE could believe it would happen again. But with a terrible inevitability the New Year once again ushered in the news that no one wanted to hear.

All-round veteran entertainer Bruce Forsyth had not been given a knighthood in the New Year's Honours List. All over Britain, the country was asking, "How could this be allowed to happen? Why didn't the government step in? Where was Tony Blair?"

Hammy Ass

A huge petition, with over one million signatures, was quickly drawn up and submitted to Downing Street urging immediate action to remedy the disaster.

Mass demonstrations outside Buckingham Palace threatened to turn nasty as furious protestors burned effigies of the hated Sir Nicholas McPherson, Permanent Secretary at the Treasury, who had been knighted whilst the more deserving Brucie had been cruelly ignored.

Said the United Nations spokesman, "The world must not sit back and watch this injustice continue. It is time for the major powers to step in and force Gordon Brown to sit down to talks with Brucie's people."

Representatives of Brucie issued a simple and moving statement to the world on behalf of Not Sir Bruce, "Knight to see me, to see me knight!"

'SOMETHING IS HAPPENING'

by Our Man Not In Gaza **MILES A. WAY**

Israel, Monday

From where I am standing it is absolutely clear that something or other is going on just over the horizon in Gaza.

I can see quite clearly a pillar of smoke rising up into the sky, which is a sure sign that there has been some sort of bombardment, possibly with bombs – and either Hamas or the Israeli army are doing something over there.

Clueless In Gaza

I can't say exactly which targets are being hit or not because I am not being allowed to get anywhere near whatever it is that is happening.

However, from my vantage point here in the bar of the Tel Aviv Ramada Inn, I *can* say that the service is very slow and *(cont. p. 94)*

THE BOOK OF EHUD

Chapter 94

1. And, lo, it came to pass that the days were accomplished that the ceasefire should end between the children of Israel and the Hamas-ites, they that dwelt in the land of Gaza.

2. And thus, as was foretold, the Hamas-ites once again sent forth into the land of Israel many rockets that are called Qassam and Faj-3 and BM-21 Grad, even unto the cities of Askelon, Ashdod and Beersheba.

3. Then Ehud that is called Olmert waxed wroth, and summoned unto him Ehud that is called Barak, who waxed even wrother.

4. And he also called Tzipi, the daughter of Livni, who waxed even wrother still.

5. And they said among thmselves, "The hour is upon us. Now is the time for smiting, as we have done so many times before, to bring peace to the land of Israel."

6. And they wagged their heads wisely, saying, "Yea, as it worked before in the land of Lebanon, when we smote the Hezboll-ites, so it will worketh again."

7. "Furthermore," they muttereth privily. "there is an election coming up, and the children of Israel tendeth to choose the ones who do the most smiting."

8. And so it came to pass that, while the Gaza-ites were watching their televisions by night, behold, the skies were filled with a heavenly host raining bombs on them and singing "No peace on earth, ill will to men."

9. And, as the fire and brimstone decended on the Gaza-ites, they were slain in their hundreds, even men, women and children.

10. And in the streets of the city of Gaza there was much wailing and gnashing of teeth.

11. And Ehud cried aloud, saying, "Verily, that will teach you Hamas-ites to launch your rockets at the land of Israel."

12. And the Hamas-ites laughed him to scorn, and launched more rockets into the land of Israel where the people were also slain but not in quite the same numbers.

13. If thou wouldst not know the score, looketh away now.

14. Which is what most of the world did.

15. The score was as follows: Gaza-ites – 400; Israel-ites – 4.

16. Which is an good result.

17. And Ehud said, "Behold, this showeth that the smiting is working. Never again will we see the rockets of the Hamas-ites darkening the skies of Israel... hangeth on, what is that falling from the heavens... ?"

18. And as he spake there was an mighty boom, like unto the thunder that fills even the mighty Leviathan with dread as he slumbereth off the coast of Eilat (which currently offereth three weeks for the price of one, hurry, hurry, hurry, while Israel lasts).

19. Then, as the smoke cleareth, Ehud saith, "Right. That's done it. There is only one way to stop this kind of thing. More smiting!" And the children of Israel rejoiced, saying, "Too true, Ehud. For there be-eth only one language that these people of Gaza understandeth."

20. So Ehud sent forth a mighty army and tanks, even an hundredfold, to carry out the next round of smiting that would finally bring lasting peace to the land of Israel.

21. Just as it hath done so many times before.

22. And, lo, the war continued, even unto the twenty-second day.

23. And Ehud looked upon it and saw that it was good.

24. Then said Ehud, son of Olmert, "Let us *now* declare an cease-fire.

25. "For, lo, we have achieved our objective.

26. "Which was to get a quick war in before Obama cometh.

27. "For Barack, son of Obama, may not looketh so kindly on our smiting as did Dubya, that is called the Burning Bush."

28. And so it came to pass that the smiting ceased.

29. And the children of Israel said to themselves, "Great is Ehud for he hath prevailed over the Hamas-ites."

30. But the Hamas-ites, as ye mighteth expect, said to *themselves,* "Great is Hamas for we have prevailed over the might of Israel."

31. And all the nations of the world talketh amongst themselves, saying, "Something must be done – though quite *what,* we knoweth not what it is."

(To be continued)

Christmas brings the traditional Slaughter of the Innocents

UN SAYS 'WORLD UNITED' OVER GAZA

by Our International Staff **Luke Theotherway**

AFTER meeting in an emergency session, the UN has issued a communiqué saying that the world is united in its determination to do nothing in the face of Israel's continuing attack on Gaza.

"In past conflicts between the Israelis and the Palestinians in the region, there has been some wavering in the international community's commitment to looking the other way, but this time, they are united in their determination to *(cont. p. 94)*

Fortean Times

Woman Claims To Have Seen 'Little Green Shoots'

by Our UFO Staff **Andrew Mars**

EXPERTS were baffled last night when a British woman, Shriti Vadera, claimed that she had seen "green shoots" appearing in the UK economy.

On Another Planet

Said Ms Vadera, "I saw a mysterious light at the end of the tunnel and then these little green shoots appeared."

She continued, "I know it sounds crazy, but they were really there and I experienced a strange sensation of wellbeing. The shoots seemed to have a message for us that everything was going to turn out ok."

Sceptics, however, were quick to pour scorn on Ms Vadera's sighting. Said Professor Vince Cable from *The Sky TV At Night*, "There is no evidence for the existence of UFOs – Unidentified Financial Opportunities – and I'm afraid that this sad woman has been fabricating these stories in order to draw attention to herself.

Outer Waste of Space

"What she may have seen," he conceded, "is a little Brown man telling her to go and find some good news."

"And the award for Best Actress goes to..."

"I'll give it two more minutes and if there isn't any shagging, I'm pissing off"

BRITISH STAR IN EMOTIONAL US AWARDS CEREMONY

BY OUR SHOWBIZ STAFF KATE WINSLOTTS

MILLIONS of Americans watched in awe last night as a British actor accepted the most prestigious show-business honour America has to offer.

Awarding the Presidential Medal of Freedom to his old friend Tony Blair, President Bush announced that this high honour was given to the former British premier for "Best Supporting Role In The Invasion Of Iraq" (2003).

Plainly overcome with embarrassment and wishing he wasn't there, Blair was barely able to speak as the President placed the medal around his neck.

Golden Global War

The cynical Washington press corps could not believe their eyes. "In all my years reporting these ceremonies," said one seasoned veteran, Hiram J. Toadburger of the *Cincinnati Bee*, "I have never seen a man make such a fool of himself."

Full story and pictures 8-14

Exclusive to the Sun

WOMAN 'BORN WITH TWO BREASTS'

JOURNALISTS were last night hailing a medical miracle after reports were confirmed that a woman had been born with two breasts.

The woman, who turned up to an awards ceremony wearing a skimpy dress, was featured very heavily in all newspapers.

Sub-editors have welcomed the development, saying the chances of a woman being born with two breasts can be as small as 99.999%.

2
THE TIMES

Is Matthew Parris Straight? asks Tintin

FOR years it has been assumed that the boyish reporter with the funny hair is gay – but surely, says Tintin, this is to miss all the obvious signs **94**

WORLD LEADERS UNITE TO CONDEMN 'OUTRAGE'

by Our Entire Staff

ANGER. Outrage. Disbelief. These were just some of the words being used last night to describe the universal reaction to the shocking event which has rocked the civilised world to its foundations.

From all the four corners of the earth came a swelling chorus of protest against what one world leader called "a crime against humanity without parallel in our time".

Harry, Harry While Royal Family Lasts

At the heart of the world crisis was a home-made video, showing a beaming Prince Harry referring to a fellow officer as "my little Paki friend".

News of this astonishing outburst quickly spread around the entire globe, sparking protest demonstrations in places as far afield as Tehran, Pitcairn and Tierra del Fuego.

In Pakistan, a mob several thousand strong burned down the British Embassy, while in Gaza, supporters of Hamas vented their fury at Prince Harry by firing rockets into Jerusalem.

Just Wild About Harry

At the United Nations in New York, an emergency meeting of the Security Council passed a resolution unanimously condemning the Prince's remarks, calling for him to withdraw immediately and face charges of genocidal hatred before the International Criminal Court.

Also quick to condemn the Prince was **Vladimir Putin**, the Czar Of All The Russians, who turned off all gas supplies to Europe in protest, warning that they would not be reconnected again until the bill was paid.

What A Harry-On

Another world statesman quick to deplore the Prince's outburst was Zimbabwean President **Robert Mugabe**, who declared, "This is yet further proof that Britian has descended into a new Dark Ages, where its unelected leaders murder people openly in the streets".

In St Peter's Square, Rome, millions of pilgrims heard **Pope Benedict XVI** proclaiming that his "heart was saddened by the news of this shameful and blasphemous outburst". He called upon all Christians throughout the world to join in prayer for the Prince's redemption from "such a grievous sin".

President-elect **Obama**, however, declined to comment, stating that as soon as he entered the White House it would be at the top of his priorities.

Prince Harry is 19.

"Er…darling, the tattooist's arrived"

Letters to the Editor

Prince Harry

From Sir Herbert Gussett.

Sir, As one who has served in the Armed Forces as a regular soldier, I find it extraordinary that anyone should take offence at the type of harmless, good-natured barrack-room banter which would be only too familiar to anyone who has had the privilege of taking the Queen's (or, as it was in my day, King's) Shilling.

I well remember the time when I was serving in the Western Desert in 1942, when the Eighth Army was kicking Rommel for six. I can see still see my old comrades' faces in my mind's eye as clearly as if they were standing before me now – Lieutenant "Chalky" Black, Major "Poofy" Huffington, Captain "Lofty" Smallbottom, and our irrepressible and much-loved colleague from India, Prince "Nig-Nog" Brahmaputra. Indeed even I had my own affectionate sobriquet, "Snorter" Gussett, a reference I believe to my fondness for knocking back the odd dram or two, which of course in those dark times were few and far between.

But let me stress that there was nothing remotely offensive in the use of these playful "noms-de-guerre", which only occasionally gave rise to acts of violence between us.

Prince Harry should be saluted for keeping alive one of the oldest and most honourable of our military traditions.

SIR HERBERT GUSSETT (Maj. Gen. Retd), The Old Khazi, Bagshot, Beds.

From Mr Michael Giggler.

Sir, I've got some advice for Prince Harry. Why don't you "Paki-tin"?

MIKE GIGGLER (Via email).

"When I said 'Dance!', Kincaid, I didn't mean contemporary"

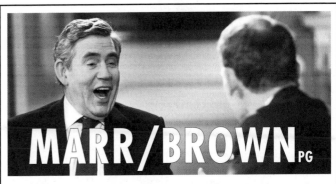

YES, HE'S BACK – AND BOLDER THAN EVER!

That Jonathan Ross/Tom Cruise Interview In Full

(Studio band "Four Poofs and a Piano" sing "Wossy's Back In Town", as Ross bounds onto stage. Hysterical applause as studio audience see themselves on TV monitors)

Jonathan Ross *(for it is he)*: Thank you, thank you, thank you! I'd just like to start by apologising... for this show. No, but sewiously – tonight we have the very gweat honour to welcome one of the vewy gweatest human beings of all time – the movie stars' movie star – none other than Mr Tom Cwuise.

(Hysterical applause as beaming Scientologist climbs out of space ship and walks onto set)

Ross: Welcome! Tom, you're twuly fantastic in your new film, as you have been in all your other films. Tom, I have the feeling that you're the sort of person who, when he sets out to do something, he weally does it.

Cruise *(nodding and smiling)*: Yeah, I guess so.

(More hysterical applause

from audience, as the "Four Poofs" dance around the piano in ecstasy)

Ross: I mean, you're the sort of person who, if I ask you a question, you'll weally focus on answering it.

Cruise: Yeah, that's right.

Ross: Now, this amazing new film of yours "Valkyrie" is about Hitler, and what everyone wants to know is – did the Führer fart in the bunker?

(Audience explodes with hysterical laughter at Wossy's cutting-edge wit. All four Poofs carried out on piano lid after fainting with amusement)

Cruise: Well, hey, I guess I just don't know. But he was certainly one helluva guy!

Ross: Tom Cwuise, it's been a pwivilege and honour to have you on the pwogwamme.

(More hysterical applause from audience, as the legendary star re-enters spaceship and flies back to scientology conference in East Grinstead. [Surely the planet Theta? Ed])

Why You Won't Read In The Daily Mail

Why Oh Why Are We Selling Off Our National Heritage To Dodgy Foreigners?

asks Leading Historian SIR MAX HASTINGS

THE SPANIARDS own our airports. The Indians own our steel industry. The French own our water and electricity.

And now, to cap it all, one of Britain's most prestigious newspapers, the world-famous London Evening Standard, is to be flogged off for a pittance to a former agent of the once-hated Russian KGB.

You couldn't make it up. What has got into the heads of the owners of this hugely respected icon of British journalism that they can so casually hand it over to a shady spy-turned-oligarch?

Reds Under Lebedev

Have the Standard's owners no shame, as they trample on 180 years of proud British reporting, in the name of turning a squalid penny – or should we say Moscow gold?

Just consider what we are witnessing here. A newspaper long famous for its conservative views and traditional British principles will henceforth be the puppet and plaything of a Communist agent whose only concern will be to further the advance of Russian interests across the globe.

And who was responsible for this act of gross national betrayal?

Step forward the craven and cringeing figure of Jonathan Harmsworth, the 3rd Viscount Rothermere, whose grandfather grovelled to Hitler, and who now appears to be keeping up the family tradition by toadying to his new masters in the Kremlin.

© *World copyright Hitlertrash Productions 2009.*

THE Sun

Friday, February 6, 2009

- There's more bum in the Sun!
- Read all about tit!

U.S. KING OF SEX IS DEAD

by Our Literary Staff PHIL CONDOM

AMERICA's uncrowned "King of Sex", writer John Updike, has died at the age of 69 (surely '76'? Ed).

For 40 years his books sold in their millions, thanks to their steamy cocktail of sex and more sex in suburban small-town America.

Rabbit Blue

From the 1950s on, Updike broke down the bedroom door of prim and proper America and described in lurid and explicit detail who was doing what to whom.

Swinging... love-romps... suspenders... orgies... adultery... wife-swapping... everyone at it like rabbits... Upskirt's pen sketched all these raunchy scenes of everyday middle-class American life as no one had ever done before.

With such unforgettable sentences as "Rabbit's hot trembling fingers ripped the thin silk from her *(Cont. p. 94)*.

One, two, three, PHWOAR! Updike's unforgettable three-in-a-bed Satanic romp in *Witches Of Eastwick* rocketed Jack Nicholson to stardom

---

Nice Work If You Can Get It

COATS

NITE SPOT

No.1 Cloakroom attendant in the North-East of England

Thank you for flying US Airways. Captain Sullenberger and his crew hope you enjoyed your flight and look forward to seeing you again soon

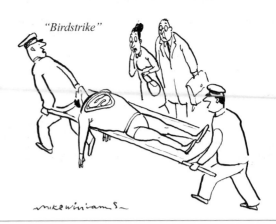

"Birdstrike"

BUSH ANNOUNCES 'WAR ON GEESE'

by Our Man In Washington **Rock Hudson-River**

IN A final speech, the outgoing President, George W. Bush, warned America that Al Qaeda-trained geese were responsible for a suicidal attack on an American passenger plane, flight 1549, which was brought down by a birdstrike after leaving New York airport.

Said the soon-to-be-ex-President, "We are going to kick goose. They can fly, but they can't hide. Er... Is it time for me to go now?"

On Other Pages
- Geese in Rendition Flight shock 2
- Geese incarcerated at Guantanamo Bay 3
- Video of Goosama Bin Laden pledging war on America 94

TOP FOOTBALLER IN 'QUIET EVENING AT HOME' SHOCK

by Our Football Staff **LUNCHTIME O'BOOTS**

THE WORLD of soccer was rocked to its foundations last night when it was revealed that a top Premiership footballer had spent an evening quietly at home with his wife and family.

"I don't know what came over me," said England striker Steve Wayne. "I got back from the game, put the kids to bed and then had supper with my wife in front of the television. It was a moment of madness."

STEVIE BLUNDER

"I know I should have been out with the lads at a club until four in the morning, getting pissed and picking fights with people."

Said a repentant Steve, "I am having therapy to talk me through the issues that confront me at this difficult phase of my life.

"I realise that if I get addicted to this lifestyle it could destroy me as a professional footballer."

■ **What do you think they should do with Steve Wayne? Should he:**

(a) be strung up?

(b) be made captain of England?

(c) Don't know.

Let us know at www.mailytelegraph.co.uk so we've got something to fill up our pages without having to pay any journalists because we've sacked them all.

New picture for Imperial War Museum

A MOVING painting of world leaders blindly stumbling forward into a global disaster, 'Gasbags' by Sir John Dancer Sergeant, has been acquired by Britain's Imperial War Museum.

Brian Sewell writes:
"With their bowed heads and downward gaze, these tragic figures convey a mood of impending despair. At the rear the Frenchman clings desperately to his British ally who himself has no idea which direction he is going. Is there a sadder image in all (cont. p94)

GLENDA SLAGG

The Gal Who Drives Away The Gloom!

■ MADONNA! Who does she think she is!?! Well past fifty and showing us her crotch yet again!?! Gor Blimey!?! As if we haven't seen it a thousand times before – and, believe me, Madge, it isn't looking any better!?! Take a tip from Auntie Glenda, dearie, put a pair of trousers on and Zimmer yourself into the Sunset Home where you belong!?!!

■ HATS OFF to Madonna?!!??! She may be past fifty but I say she puts girls half her age to shame!?! And what a crotch!?! It's never looked better – if you ask me she should keep her trousers off even when she's in the Sunset Home pushing herself round on her Zimmer!?!

■ POSH!?! Who does she think she is?! Madonna?!!?! Taking off her trousers and showing us her crotch!??! Put 'em back on, darlin', and give us all a break!!?!

■ THREE cheers for Posh – she's not afraid to take her trousers off and show us her crotch!!? No wonder Madonna is looking so crotchety (Geddit?) 'cos when it comes to showing your crotch, Posh is in a class of her own!!!?

■ *HERE THEY ARE – Glenda's Downturn Dreamboats!?!*

● **Boy George.** OK, you're in prison but you can chain me up, Big Boy (and I mean *Big*) any time!!?!

● **John McDonnell MP.** He's the gorgeous guy who grabbed the Mace in the House of Commons, stoopid!?! Mmmm!! I'd like to grab *your* mace, Johnny (Geddit?) and we can Third Runaway together!?! Geddit?!!?

● **Captain Chesley B. Sullenberger III.** Crazy name, quite a sensible guy!?!

Byeee!!

"Better move the sticker, unless you want Madonna breaking into your car"

Private Eye has decided not to run this humanitarian appeal on the grounds that we must remain impartial at all times.

THE APPEAL YOU WON'T SEE

Nursery Times

PIGS AND WOLF CRISIS

WE MUST REMAIN IMPARTIAL

IN recent days, Nursery Times has come under extensive criticism for our refusal to publish an appeal on behalf of the three little pigs, two of which lost not only their homes, but also their lives, as a result of the recent conflict in the Nursery Region involving the wolf.

The Nursery Times defends its decision on the grounds that it has a duty to remain impartial in its coverage of this crisis, under the terms of the Nursery Times Charter.

While hostilities between the two sides were at their height, we were careful not to take sides, and whilst sympathetic to the plight of the pigs, we invariably recognised the right of the wolf to put his point of view.

This is why we consistently gave space to the wolf's spokesman, who emphasised that he had been extremely hungry and had a right to huff, puff and blow down (or indeed up) any houses that he wished.

On other pages

● EU to Fund Pig Reconstruction Programme Again **14**

● Did Pigs Secretly Belong to Ham-as? *(That's enough. Ed.)*

DRAGONS TO BE REINTRODUCED TO BRITAIN

by Our Environmental Correspondent **St George Monbiot**

CONSERVATIONISTS have welcomed the decision to reintroduce dragons to the British countryside, where they have been extinct for over 1,000 years.

"We are delighted that the dragon is back among us," said a spokesman for the Ancient World Wildlife Fund.

"Once again, this beautiful and iconic creature is free to roam our woods and

fields, breathing fire and devouring maidens."

The dragon's reintroduction has been funded by the EU, as part of its 2-billion-Euro Bio-Diversity and Encouragement of Tourism In Remote Areas Programme.

HEADLINES 'GLOOMIEST SINCE YESTERDAY'

by Our Economics Staff **Phil Job-Centre**

BRITAIN's headlines were officially declared as "depressing" after they had been gloomy for two quarters running.

"Yesterday's headlines were lowering enough," said a Treasury spokesman, "but today's have hit a new level of misery.

"The fears are that tomorrow's headlines will be the worst since records began," he continued.

"There are no signs of less depressing headlines and it may be years before we see any sort of recovery in *(cont. p. 94)*

Those Depressing Headlines In Full

Recession Worst Since 1980s, says IMF	**Recession Worst Since Dark Ages, says Darling**
Recession Worst Since 2nd World War, says CBI	**Recession Worst Since Great Flood Destroyed Life on Earth, says Mervyn King**
Recession Worst Since 1920s, says Treasury	
Recession Worst Since Black Death, says Balls	**Government Worst Since Beginning of Time, says everyone**

BABY HAS FATHER WHO IS YOUNGER THAN HE IS

by Our Broken Britain Staff
Max Clifford Hastings

Father: Darren

IN A shocking indictment of modern-day Britain, a baby was born yesterday to a father who is *(cont. pp 2, 3, 4, 5, 6, 7, & 94)*

'I WAS JOHN LENNON,' Claims Paul McCartney

by Our Pop Correspondent
John Paul George and Ringo Sartre

IN AN amazing outburst that has rocked the world of popular music, Sir Paul McCartney has revealed that he was the anti-war political thinker and activist in the Beatles.

Said Sir Paul, "People have got it wrong. It wasn't John who was the serious one, writing songs about war and revoulation and that. It was, like me, Macca.

"John hadn't even heard of Vietnam and the bomb until I wrote *'Ob-La-Di, Ob-La-Da, Life goes on, Whoa!'*.

The world's greatest ever living composer went on to prove his point by showing some previously unseen songs which he penned after being inspired by meeting the late Bertrand Russell on a CND march in 1958.

Macca's Political Pop Songs That Would Have Changed The World

● **Eleanor Roosevelt**
● **We don't want to live in a Trident submarine**
● **When I'm 1968**
● **Killing Fields Forever**
● **Political Paperback Writer (E.P. Thompson)**
● **Imagine (I'm John Lennon)**

"I'm sorry Mr Escher, but yes, you will have to fit disabled access"

POWER-SHARING AGREEMENT

I'll have the power

And I'll share the cell...

Duchess of Love

by DAME SYLVIE KRIN, author of *Born To Be Queen,*
Heir Of Sorrows and *You're Never Too Old.*

*THE STORY SO FAR:
Prince Charles is feeling
low after the excitement of
his 60th birthday has worn
off. Now read on...*

"IT REALLY is
appalling..." Charles
flung down his freshly-
ironed copy of the Daily Mail,
upsetting his row of six boiled
eggs and buttered soldiers
made from stoneground
wholewheat locally sourced
bread.

Camilla raised an eyebrow
as she scanned the *Racing
Post*'s list of runners in the
Queen Mother's Statue Cup at
Cheltenham. "What's
appalling this time?" she
asked, lighting a Trident Full
Strength untipped.

"Listen to this," Charles
spluttered. "Some professor
chap has had the flaming
bloody cheek to say that my
Duchy Detox Elixir, made
from handpicked nettles and
fresh celery is, and I quote,
'Of no use whatsoever and
could even be dangerous'."

Camilla blew out an
exquisitely formed smoke ring
which hovered above Charles'
boiled eggs like an unearthly
halo.

"Calm down, Chazza," she
soothed. "Your face has gone
the colour of the raspberry
jam."

Charles harrumphed
furiously. "I mean, one does
one's best, you know, to help
people who are poisoning
themselves with these toxin
thingies. You take that fat girl
in the village who works in the
shop where you get your
cigarettes, I mean, she must
be terribly unhealthy.
Someone's got to help her and
a good dose of nettles and
celery could wash away all
those chips and crisps and
chocolate pie thingies."

"Really, Chazza," Camilla
countered. "It's only a
gimmick with your Duchy
brand. Duchy this, Duchy
that... they've even got it in
Waitrose now."

Charles banged his egg
spoon down furiously. "*No.
No.* It actually works. And
since we're being frank, old
girl, it wouldn't do you any
harm to have a detox either."

Camilla groaned. She knew
all too well what was coming.

"In fact, I'm going to ring up
Barkworth from the Duchy
now to get him to send a bottle
round and you're going to take
some. And don't pull that face."

With that, Charles looked
at his watch and hurried
towards the door.

"Damn it! I'm going to be
late for my interfaith prayer
morning with Imam
Rabinowitz and Rabbi bin
Laden."

CAMILLA STOOD in the
oak-panelled Duke of
Ellington drawing
room and looked warily at the
green bottle Barkworth had
delivered. She took a tentative
swig from it and instantly spat
it out. God, it was disgusting,
she thought, like the medicine
Nanny Mainwaring used to
make her drink in the nursery
when she had a tummy ache.

Well, she wasn't drinking any
of *that* muck!

Without thinking, Camilla
emptied the whole bottle into
the flowering Columbian
Anaconda which stood in a
marble pot under Charles'
favourite watercolour *"Donkey
by Moonlight – Near Cairo
1981".*

Too late, she realised what
she had done and she could
already hear Charles' voice as
he came through the door
telling Fitztightly to take his
wellington boots off and "be
smart about it".

What could she do? Any
minute now he would be
wanting to test his tincture!
But suddenly she had an
inspired idea...

Charles threw himself
into his Louis Walsh
XIV chair and sighed
heavily.

"What a day! I thought the
Imam would never stop. And
as for the Dalai Lama for
goodness sake... By the way,
old girl, did that Duchy
tincture come? I could
certainly do with a shot of it.
Those toxin chaps are playing
merry havoc with old Chazza's
insides."

Camilla sprang to her feet
and presented him with a
silver tray on which stood
ready the green bottle and two
Waterstone crystal goblets – a
present from Sir Tony
O'Looney, the Irish
entrepreneur, after a
fascinating Royal visit to the
workshop in County Kilroy.

Charles beamed with
pleasure as Camilla poured
out two full measures of the
translucent fluid.

"It says on the bottle,
Chazza, patients should down
it in one."

"Really...? It is usually to be
taken in very small doses
three times a day..."

"Not this one. Bottoms up!"
Camilla insisted. Charles did
as he was told, gulping down
the proffered tincture.

"Phew! Gosh! You know, it
tastes a bit like... gin. Quite a
kick."

Camilla's eyes wandered
back to the half-empty bottle
of Gordon's Bankers' Ruin on
top of the drinks cabinet.

"Yes, I thought so too," she
agreed. Charles relaxed,

suffused with a warm glow,
and the thoughts of his
difficult day receded. He
contentedly wiggled his toes
in his Royal monogrammed
Duchy slippers.

"Tell you what, old bean, I
think I might have another of
those Cettles and Nelery
Elixir thingies. Mmm... you
see, those professorsh don't
know what they're talking
about. This stuff is bloody
marvelloush."

What was it his old friend
and mentor Sir Laurens Van
Der Post had said that night
under the Rumbabwe Desert
sky? "A little bit of what you
fancy does you good." How
true that was, how very true
that was.

(To be continued...)

Those Israeli Election Results In Full

Armageddon North

Livni Letdie (Smiting For Peace Party) **4,703**; **Menachem Beginthewaragain** (More Smiting And Less Peace Party) **4,406**; **Rabbi Solomon Ben Looni** (Build More Walls Now/Even More Smiting Alliance) **2,304**; **Letzbi Frenz** (Socialist No Hope Of Winning Party) **12**.

(No change)

Jericho South

Louis Armstrongstein (Trumpeters Against Walls) **13**; **Rabbi Satchmoses** (cont. p. 94)

"I'm just calling to check if you'd got my letter about the email I sent you?"

CONRAD BLACK'S PLEA FOR A PARDON
What George Bush Won't Read (Because He Can't)

Dear Mr President,

I believe it was Talleyrand who first expressed the view that an innocent imprisoned man was, in the words of Montaigne, like a multi-plumed, exotic songbird trapped in a cruel iron cage, an allegory that is singularly apposite in my own case, which is that of the most unjust incarceration in the history of United States jurisprudence and wherewithal I solemnly submit (continued for 94 years in jail)

Jamie Oliver's Ministry Of Swearing

Recipe Sheet No. 94

To Start
Fuck Soup

– ✳ –

Main
Spaghetti Bollocknaise

– ✳ –

Sweet
Bread & Bugger Pudding

– ✳ –

To Finish
Crappuccino

BELGIANS INVENTED CROQUET SHOCK

by Our Sports Correspondent **Timmy Mallett**

RECENT evidence unearthed by an Australian academic, **Professor Bruce McPossum from the University of Hullaballoo in New South Wales**, proves that the game of croquet originated not in England but in Bruges in Belgium.

According to a poem he has discovered by the little known Walloon poet, Erik Van der Thribb, writing in the 17½th century, croquet was already played by Bruges emigrant weavers working in Essex in the fast-emerging Trouser Press Industry.

The poem reads:
Hët die ball
Thruwen die hoop
And listen ye all
To the cheers of die Grüpe

Says the professor, "This is clearly proof that croquet is nothing to do with the bloody poms who are as useless at croquet as they are at cricket, rugby and everything else. Mine's a large glass of the amber."

CROQUET LATEST
England   93 all out
Belgium   793 for 3

WHITE HELL BLITZES BLIZZARD BRITAIN

What You Missed (All Channels)

John *(or it may be Eamonn)*: The time's coming up to 7.42 and there are reports of severe weather conditions all over Britain. So over to Denise at the Weather Centre...

Denise *(for it is she)*: The Met Office has issued a severe snow event warning for all parts of Britain and travellers are advised to stay at home unless your journey is absolutely necessary. Back to you now, John.

John: Thank you, Denise. So, the message from the Met Office warns of a severe snow event. And their advice is that, unless your journey is absolutely necessary, you should stay at home. And now over to the Travel Centre for an update on Britain's roads.

Andy Divot, Roads Spokesman

Divot: Well, John, I'm not at the Travel Centre because I've heeded the snow event warnings on the news and I've stayed at home. And here in Chipping Norton where I live it's quite pleasant, actually, and if I look out of the window, I can just see the traffic moving quite freely on the A40, but my wife's just told me she's heard on the radio that there's severe disruption on the railways due to the snow event.

John: Thanks, Andy. And we'll come back to you later when, hopefully, there'll be a serious snow event in your part of the world. And, unfortunately, we can't give you an update on rail travel because the website's crashed due to excessive demand. But we've just had this text from Vince, a container lorry driver between junctions 26 and 27 on the M25, and he tells us that the traffic flow is unusually good due to everybody heeding the warning to stay at home. Thank you, Vince. And keep those texts and emails coming in. And the time's coming up to to 7.52 and if you've been wondering how Britain's otters cope with something like a major snow event, here in the studio we have global warming guru Professor Barkworth whose book *'The Snow Otter'* has just been published. Professor, could I start by asking you how you got in today.

Barkworth: Well, it was quite easy really *(cont. Channel 94)*

PABLO PICASSO FACE PAINTER

Lookalikes

Laurel　　　　**Sarkozy**

Sir,

Sacre bleu! Quel etonnant resemblance entre M. Nicolas Sarkozy, le mari du fameuse stunner Italienne Carla Bruni, et le comique anglais Stan Laurel. Mon dieu, est ce que c'est possible que Stan Laurel est actuellement le grandpere du Nicolas? Zut alors! Cela could expliquer bien pourquoi la France est dans un autre fine mess!

PETER REYNOLDS,
Birmingham.

Paisley　　　　**Pope**

Sir,

Could Ian Paisley be a reincarnation of the Pope Innocent X as seen by Francis Bacon (after Velasquez)?

ENA B. ANONYMOUS,

Via email.

Meerkat　　　　**Radio 4's Evan Davis**

Sir,

With the latest revelations regarding human origins, perhaps we should now claim to be descended from a really interesting member of the animal kingdom: the Meerkat, say.

GORDON PETHERBRIDGE,
North Bucks.

Salmond　　　　**Shrek**

Sir,

Has anybody spotted our first minister at Holyrood?

ARCHIE SHAW STEWART,
Doune, Perthshire.

Wood　　　　**Plastic**

Sir,

Whilst browsing the popular online car boot sale eBay™, I came across the following elderly second-hand plaything for the young and wondered if it could have been modelled from life?

Best wishes,
ALASDAIR SWANSON,

Via email.

Golly　　　　**Stephens**

Sir,

Don't know if you spotted it on Tuesday night's BBC News about Carol Thatcher's "offensive" golliwog comment, but the guy they wheeled out to condemn her cruel comments (some human rights lawyer, I think [Mark Stephens. Ed.]) had the most perfect vertical hair, starting halfway back on his head.

If ever anyone had hair like the famous strawberry jam maker it was this guy, and he was saying how bad it was for her to describe people as golliwogs. We just howled!

Regards,
DAVID YOUNG,

Via email.

Washington　　　　**Madoff**

Sir,

Has anyone else noticed the resemblance between Bernard Madoff and the portrait of George Washington on the One Dollar bill? Could this be a subliminal reason why so many people trusted him with their money?

Yours,
OLIVER MAUDE-ROXBY,

London SW1.

Churchill　　　　**Curtis**

Sir,

Is this indeed Tony Curtis, the well-known Hollywood star of yesteryear, or a rare photo of our very own Winston Churchill in a Stetson?

DAVE HOWELL,

Via email.

Rickman　　　　**Gaddafi**

Sir,

Surely I am not alone in noting the more-than-passing resemblance of respected thespian Muammar al-Gaddafi and "Brotherly Leader and Guide of the Revolution" Alan Rickman?

F.S. WANLESS,

Nottingham.

Doll　　　　**Thatcher**

Sir,

I cannot help but notice the uncanny resemblance between Carol Thatcher and a rag doll.

I think that the Iron Lady owes us an apology.

Yours,
SANDY GEMMILL,

Edinburgh.

Dancer　　　　**Cardinal**

Sir,

I couldn't help noticing the incredible resemblance between Stanislaw Cardinal Dziwisz, Archbishop of Krakow, and recently resigned dancer John Sergeant. Are they by any chance related?

NICHOLAS PADDEN-DUNCAN,

Via email.

Sontaran   **George**

Sir;
    I was struck by the similarity of disgraced DJ Boy George and this inter-galactic baddie – a Sontaran – from the Dr Who series.
    Perhaps, upon his release, BJ could do a screen test as one of them? I mean, the make-up department wouldn't have to do much!

        Yours,
        DONNY COUTTS,

Via email.

Mandelson   **Hawtrey**

Sir;
    I wonder if anyone else has noticed the increasing similarity between the now bespectacled Peter Mandelson and the late bespectacled comic actor Charles Hawtrey, the man who played Private Widdle.

        Yours,
        ALAN WHITING,
Via email.

Davis   **Goodwin**

Sir;
    I wonder if in his many private jet flights with Sir Fred Goodwin, Lord Gnome has noticed how uncannily he resembles that master of the green baize, Steve Davis. Perhaps he will also have compared their abilities to pocket everything they can and snooker everyone else.

        JOE DONNELLY,

Via email.

Murray   **Werewolf**

Sir;
    I hope your readers will join me in demanding an unreserved apology from the ATP for such insensitive scheduling of Andy Murray's fourth-round tie. Playing late at night under a full moon obviously affected him adversely...
        MAX PETROKOFSKY,
Via email.

Wallace   **McCain**

Sir;
    Nick Park has a lot to answer for, methinks.
        MEILIR PAGE,
Renton, Washington, USA.

Bruce   **Basil**

Sir;
    The veteran TV presenter Bruce Forsyth – that wily old fox and presenter of Strictly Come Dancing – has been exposed to many foxy ladies in various attire. Is he perhaps related to the ultimate vulpine host, Basil Brush?
    There is no need to ring back; lines are now closed.

        Yours in the dugout,
        GRAHAM DALLAS,

Via email.

"La Chata"   **Winehouse**

Sir;
    The popular media would have us believe that Amy Winehouse is 25 years old. But on a recent trip to Barcelona, I visited the Picasso Museum and stumbled cross irrefutable evidence that she is, in fact, **at least** 110.

        Yours,
        ROB BERNARD SMITH,
Birmingham.

Saunders   **McBride**

Sir;
    Can you see the resemblance between Damian McBride and the gross, drunken, sex-obsessed man played by Jennifer Saunders?
        SHAUN ROLPH,
Via email.

Gest   **Jones**

Sir;
    I hope it's not unusual, and others can see the similarities between these two icons of our times.

        Yours,
        GUY HALL,
Via email.

Terfel   **Balls**

Sir;
    Please print this one, it would make me insanely happy.
        IRENA BARKER,
Via email.

Kim   **Anne**

Sir;
    While watching Scotland play a recent Rugby Union International at Murrayfield, I was surprised to see the bouffant-haired Dear Leader of North Korea Kim Jong-il in the Royal Box. Usually it is our beloved Princess Royal in the dark glasses – maybe she was opening a bridge in North Korea.

        SCOTT A. KEIR
Via email.

Zombie   **Chiles**

Sir;
    While playing a new video game (House of the Dead: Overkill) on my Wii, I was very surprised to find the majority of the zombies I was killing were modelled upon Adrian Chiles from BBC One's One Show. A fate many of us wish upon him?

        RHYS ROBERTS,
Anglesey.

Bafta Frocks Shocks!

IT'S THE BAFTAS AGAIN... and our fashion editor **LIZ SLAGG** gives us her usual round-up of the gowns that made her frown and the frocks that rocked her world!

This blowsy gown is a real dumble-bore! If **Emily** wants to show us the snape of her womanly curves she need to go the whole hog – warts and all!

Miss Watson's slinky number shows a body that just won't quidditch! I bet all the boy wizards will want to Pot-her in this one!

Fancy an Indian? Not in this fussy gown – you wouldn't give it to a slumdog! **Freida** needs a millionaire to buy her a proper outfit.

The 'Millionaire' star shows us some real Tarrant in this stunning fairytale frock! The designer deserves to be serenaded with "Freida jolly good fellow!"

What a SS-exy number, eh readers! This Revolutionary Road outfit will get the men's heads spinning!

I don't want to be Nazi but what a terrible frock! More of a Revolutionary Road Crash, **Kate**!

(That's enough. Ed.)

LORDS 'CASH FOR INFLUENCE' SCANDAL

by Our Political Staff **Lunchtime O'Sleaze**

A PROMINENT member of the House of Lords, Lord Gnome, today angrily denied that he had been prepared to change the laws of the land on behalf of a lobbying organisation.

Gnome was one of a number of peers targeted by journalists from a Sunday newspaper who had posed as businessmen wanting to buy "influence" in the House of Lords.

The journalists taped Lord Gnome in a three-hour conversation in the House of Lords bar, the highlights of which we reproduce below.

But yesterday, faced with the evidence of the tapes, Lord Gnome angrily denied that he had done anything wrong. He claimed that his recorded words had been taken out of context and misquoted to make it look as if he was "some kind of a sleazy crook who was up to no good."

THAT GNOME TAPE IN FULL

Journalist: So you can get the law changed, can you?

Gnome: I don't want to boast, but I have a lot of influence around this place and, if I have a couple of words with the right people, you can be sure that we'll get the result you want. Wheels within wheels, old boy!

Journalist: So how much do you want?

Gnome: Money is not important to me. This is a matter of great national importance. What was it about again? Anyway, no matter. But were you to mention the sum of, say, £1 million, you would be about in the right area. I do a lot of this sort of work. I've been around this place for a long time.

Journalist: So let's be clear about this, and can you speak a little bit closer to my tie? We give you the cash and you get the law changed the way we want. Is that right?

Gnome: Absolutely, my friend. That's what I'm here for. So why don't we celebrate by you chaps buying me lunch? The Caprice is awfully good these days...

From The Message Boards

Members of the online community respond to the major issues of the day...

Gay ducks won't mate with sole remaining female

The Arundel Wetland Centre did no more than bring in the two male blue ducks to mate with the only female to save the species from extinction. But the males did no more than ignore the female and court one another. Inasmuch and insofar as they did so do, then they did no more than Onan, who did no more than spill his seed on the ground. – *Mr Salmon*

Wildlife experts agree that homo-sexuality is rife in the duck community. It is, in effect, "natural". But would it kill them to mate with this female just once? Do they not realize that their selfish attitude means there will be no more gay ducks either? One of them will live to regret his short-sightedness, when his partner dies and there are no gay males left. – *Robert "R"*

i sed it befor wen there was the book with the gay pengin's bring-ing up the baby pengin an then the reel life gay pengin's in the zoo got marryd an adopt-ed the abandend baby pengin's 😊 now the duck's r gay 2😊 its not natral an its spread-ing like wild flower – *Darling_Deneyze*

them duck's want shootin 😡😡 our boys come home FROM iraque TOO this!! – *Red_White_and_True*

agree 1000 persent redwite 😭 funny how the muslim fanatic's ar'nt protesting about "THIS" 😡😡 they say they are against homosexialty "BUT" there happy for english duck's to go gay and extinct. it wuld be a difrent story if the duck's was muslim's from pakistarn. – *Broken_Britan*

the lady ducks self-steam must be so low she is the only fe-male in the country and she cant get a donald duck 😟 – *Hunny_pot*

gorden brown set's the worse example 😠 in the paper it say's ther was a lesb-ien hen night at number 10 downing's street? so now the hen's r goin lesb-ien an the duck's r goin gay? soon ther wil b no duck's to eat an no egg's 2 eat 😠 an even gay human's need 2 eat? – *Hayley_321*

i dont get it? brick obama won in the electing "BUT" gorden brown is stil in charge? – *Yummy_Mummy8*

POST   BEWARE OF THE TORTOISE

THE TIMES (ROMAN)

VENERIS, FEBRUARIUS XXII, AD XXXII

CHRISTIAN PUNISHED FOR SAYING PRAYERS WHILST HEALING SICK

by Our Health Staff **Phil Istine** and **Sam Aritan**

A MIDDLE-AGED Christian man who offered prayers to accompany his healing mission was yesterday reprimanded by the authorities.

Mr Jesus Christ, 32, was alleged to have used prayer "inappropriately" on a number of occasions including incidents involving leprosy, blindness, and resurrection from the dead.

Said Mr Pontius Pilate, Head of the Regional Authority, "This is a pagan country and you really should keep your Christian beliefs to yourself."

Mr Christ was then suspended on a cross outside the city and *(That's enough blasphemy, Ed.)*

Let's Parlez Franglais!

Numero 94 Le Top-Level EU Summit

Berlusconi *(pour c'est lui)*: Saluta Sarko!

Sarkozy *(pour c'est lui)*: Bonjour Berlo! J'ai un très exciting new hobby, mon ami.

Berlo: Qu'est-ce que c'est?

Sarko: C'est le philately.

Berlo: Qué?

Sarko: C'est à dire le stamp collecting! Maintenant chaque soir je vais au lit et look at mon grand collection de beautiful timbres.

Berlo: Non e possible! Buffoni! Pullez the other jambe!

Sarko: Non, c'est vrai! C'est très interesting et grande fun!

Berlo: Mais je gather que vous avez un très valuable Italian Bruni dans votre collection – en perfect condition et

"unused" – nudgez, nudgez, winkez, winkez!!

Sarko: Qu'est-ce que vous êtes implying?

Berlo: If c'était moi dans le lit avec le rare Bruni, je wouldn't be messing around avec les boring stamps! Vous must be fou! Ou probablement gai! Pas d'offence!

Sarko: Espèce de wop! Venez outside et nous sorterons this one out!

Berlo: Comme des stamps! Ha! Ha! Ha! Et je donnerai vous un licking!

© Le Late Kilometres Kington

TOP 10 BESTSELLERS

Non-Fiction

1 TV's Charles Darwin – The Greatest Genius Ever by Sir David Attenbore (BBC Books, £38.99)

2 Darwin's Bicycle – The Naturalist As Cyclist by Jolyon Voletrouser (Oxford University Press, £48.99)

3 Lady Laetitia Starborgling – The Secret Life of Darwin's Third Cousin by Professor Norman Beamer (Virago Press, £29.99)

4 Darwin's Northamptonshire – The County That Gave The World Evolution by Hilary Corby (University of Northampton, £58.99)

5 The Other Beagle – A Life Of Darwin's Dog by Sam Leith (Aspidistra Books, £9.99)

6 Darwin At Shrewsbury – The Evolution Of A Public Schoolboy by Michael Charlesworth O.S. (St Cakes' Press, £19.99)

7 Darwin's Love Poetry, edited by Daisy Darwin-Peabody, Darwin's great-great-grand-niece (Amethyst Press, £11.99)

8 Stephen Fry's Darwin by Stephen Fry (BBC Books, £19.99)

9 Darwin's Beard by Christopher Howse (Beaver Books, £25.99)

10 Was Darwin Jack The Ripper? by Colin Wilson (UFO Press, £28.99)

(That's enough Darwin books. Ed.)

All these books are available from Gnomazon for 3p

TV Tonight

The History of Christianity

Pt 94: **Faith in a Materialist Age**

Presented by CHERIE BLAIR

(Silly music. Shot of Cherie Blair in mackintosh, walking down aisle of church)

Blair: It is very hard for the church to survive when the modern world is so overwhelmingly concerned with the making of money and the consumption of goods.

(Shot of Cherie Blair running round clothes shop and filling trolley with designer items)

Blair: Nowadays, it is all too easy to be obsessed by owning things like houses and flats.

(Shot of Cherie buying huge country mansion, formerly property of Sir John Gielgud)

Blair: Our leaders seem only concerned with enriching themselves in every way they can.

(Shot of senior Catholic figure, T. Blair, running into J.P. Morgan Bank and emerging shortly afterwards with a huge sack of money)

Blair: No wonder that the Church's message of self-denial falls upon stony ground... by the way, how much am I being paid for this? I'm very busy, you know, and I've got a lot of mortgages to pay.

(More silly music)

Ends

Next week: *A History of Venality Pt. 95*

"I'm at work, you stupid cow!"

**UNIVERSITY
CHALLENGE'S
GAIL TRIMBLE**

Have you ever...
Yes.

How many...
375.

What sort of...
Antique silver Dutch
memorial spoon.

If you had to...
George III.

Do you...
The Latin for spoon is
cochleare.

Has anything amusing...
No.

Thank you very much.

NEXT WEEK: *The late Heath
Ledger – "Me and my ledger".*

GLENDA SLAGG

Fleet Street's Toxic Asset!?!!

■ COME OFF it, Fergie!?!! Who are you kidding?!! You say you only scoffed the cakes 'cos you couldn't compete with Princess Di!?! Don't make me laugh!!?! There's only one reason you ate all the pies, sweetheart, and that's 'cos you're a great big guzzle-bucket!?!! No offence, Your Duchessness!!? So put a sock in it instead of a cream bun!?!! Geddit?! And watch the pounds slip away!!?!

■ SPARE A THOUGHT for poor old Fergie!?! No wonder she had to eat herself silly when standing alongside superslim sexy Di, the Thin People's Princess!?! Who *wouldn't* tuck into a mountain of cakes topped off with a bucket of pies when you've got the sister-in-law from Hell (or *Hello!* Geddit?!) a-tauntin' and a-flauntin', a-floutin' and a-poutin' next to you in front of the world's paparazzi!?!! Get off her back Mr Pressman and let her carry on a-crunchin' and a-munchin' her cream buns in peace!?!!

■ GAIL TRIMBLE!?!! She's University Challenge's brainy boffinette who's made being clever the in-thing!?!! Mensa? Wo-mensa, more like?!? Geddit?!? Mortarboards off to you, Gail, for showing that gals today can be more than a pretty face!?!!

■ HERE'S YOUR Starter for Ten – who's the most smug self-satisfied clever clogs on the planet?!? No conferring!?! We all know the answer to this one, don't we gals?!? It's Boring Blue-Stocking Brainbox Trimble!?! Take a tip from Aunty Glenda, swotty – belt up and act dumb. You're giving us gals a bad name!?!

Byeee!!

BANG!

ABORTION CLINIC

PRO LIFE

Why are clever women so unpopular?

asks
**Mary
Ann
Bighead**

GAIL TRIMBLE, the star of University Challenge's winning team from Corpus Christi Oxford, has been vilified for being very clever.

I know how she feels. In fact I know even more about it than she does because I'm even cleverer than her. And you may not like me for saying it but it is a fact. Just one of the millions of facts that I know – and you don't.

I too went to Oxford and I have also been on University Challenge. Like Gail I found the questions far too easy and the reason I didn't answer all of them was because I didn't want to embarrass all the other not-so-clever contestants. Clever, eh?

And that is Gail's problem. She's not clever enough to realise that being too clever is not a very clever thing to be. However I do.

So I think it's pretty clear that overall I'm cleverer than Gail and that actually I won University Challenge this year – and Ms Trimble, for all her long hair and glasses and invitations to pose for *Nuts* magazine *didn't*. And what's more Jeremy Paxman fancied me a lot more too.

© Mary Ann Bighead

The Alternative Rocky Horror Common Worship Service Book

A Service of Thanksgiving For The Recession

The President: Brother and sister jobseekers, we are gathered here today to give thanks for the current meltdown of the world economy, following the collapse of the banking system, which has given us a much-needed opportunity in a very real sense to re-examine our values and refocus our lives on the things that really matter.

Jobseekers: Indeedydo!

(There shall then be a first reading from the Book of Job)

FIRST READING

"And Job was sore afflicted. Not only was his body covered with boils, but his P45 had just come through the post.

"And the Lord spake out of the mighty whirlwind and said to Job, 'After living all those years on borrowed milk and honey, thou hadst it coming to thee.'

"And Job gave thanks to the Lord for giving him a new perspective on his work/life balance."

"Here endeth the First Reading."

OFFERTORY HYMN No. 94

"There is a green shoot far away
Without a City bonus."

(During this hymn a collection will be taken for the recently unemployed [everyone])

SECOND READING

(from The Book Of The Prophet Jeremiah Clarkson)

"Woe unto ye, all ye City tosspots and merchant wankers. Ye have lost me all my money. Ye should all be strung up for there is only one language that ye understand, and it is not Hebrew.

"Dost thou gettest my meaning?"

Reader: This is the word of the Clarkson.

Congregation: Thanks be to Stig.

OFFERTORY HYMN No. 95

"Northern Rock of Ages, cleft for me.
Let me hide my savings in thee (now that you've been nationalised)."

THE PEACE

The President: Let us all give each other our business cards as a sign of hope.

(The congregation shall then exchange cards containing contact details for their new internet start-up businesses)

THE BLESSING

The President: Bless!

(The organ shall then play 'The Trumpet Voluntary Redundancy' [arr. Felix Mandelson])

New from *Boden.* Recession Chic

Dave is wearing

A blue-collar Fairtrade working mans 'Dressing Down' in Depression Black.

Baggy low-waste organic "Chipos" with no upturns.

'Conserves', canvas leisure shoes with eco-friendly green laces and soles made from recycled tyres from banned 4x4s.

Dave's Favourite Place: The front page of the Daily Telegraph

Sam is wearing

A simple all-day shift with a tightened belt.

Boots made from non-toxic sub-prime leather.

Brass necklace borrowed from Smythsons of Bond Street.

Sam likes: Standing by her man

'NO TORTURE COVER-UP' SAYS MILIBAND

by Our Rendition Staff **Phil Cells**

THE Foreign Secretary, Mr David Miliband, denied that the Americans had twisted his arm over the use of torture on terror suspects.

"I don't know what you are talking about," he said, "I am being very well treated. The Americans are very nice indeed. They are giving me everything I want while I help them with their cover-up... I mean... no... ow... sorry, let me go."

Mr Miliband then concluded the interview and a spokesman later issued a statement on his behalf.

"Mr Miliband is unable to answer further questions and considers the matter to be water under the board." *(Surely 'bridge'? Ed.)*

RECESSION – WHAT RECESSION?

Here are the gloom-busting businesses who are putting a smile back on all our faces!

❶ Chocolate Manufacturers Britain's choc eaters are eating more of their favourite comfort food than ever! In Jan-March 2009, sales of Nestlé's "Nookie" Bar increased by 7½%.

❷ Undertakers Thanks to Britain's burgeoning suicide rate, the nation's coffin makers are enjoying a record boom!

❸ Job Centres As estate agents close, Job Centres are opening in every high street, which means more jobs in Job Centres – which must be good news!

❹ Cardboard Box Manufacturers More Britons than ever are discovering the pleasures of al fresco living! Sales of ready-made, family-size cardboard dwellings are literally going through the roof.

❺ Bad Journalism As desperate newspapers vie to fill up their pages with any old rubbish like this, really terrible hackery is recording a massive 100% increase across the board.

(That's enough booming businesses.)

NEOLITHIC TIMES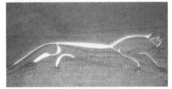

Protests Greet Giant White Horse Plan

BY OUR ARTS STAFF BRON ZAGE

How it will look

ENVIRONMENTALISTS were up in arms last night after plans were unveiled to create an enormous image of a white horse on the downs above the Berkshire village of Uffington.

"This is an outrage," said local cave-dweller Ugg Sewell, who called the horse "a grotesque eyesore which will completely ruin the view. With its ridiculously minimalist daubings, it doesn't even look like a horse.

"Quite frankly, a child of five could have done it better."

But local community leaders were enthusiastic about the design. Local councillor Wayland Smithy told the *Neolithic Times*, "I can confidently predict that the Uffington White Horse will be a terrific tourist attraction and will still be drawing crowds of visitors to the area in thousands of years' time."

What's your view on the Great White Horse Debate? Chisel your opinion now (flint on sandstone please) and send via pterodactyl to the Editor, Alan Ugsbridger.

'BAIL-OUT WORKING,' SAYS CAPTAIN

by Our Shipping Staff **Michael White Star Line**

THE CAPTAIN of the Titanic last night praised his crew's efforts to rescue his sinking ship.

Captain Brown announced from the bridge, "The bailing-out process is going according to plan. We will be bottoming out very soon and we are on course for the sea bed."

Unsinkable Gordon Brown

The Titanic recently hit a huge Northern Rock, which opened a black hole below the waterline,

and has been in trouble ever since. However Captain Brown said, "There is no cause for alarm. I will not be going down with the glug.. glug... glug...!!"

"Oh no! Illegal immigrants – thousands of 'em!"

45

Lives of the Saints and Martyrs No. 94
St Jade the Goody
(sometimes known as St Jade the Obscure)

THERE WAS in that time a poor peasant girl, ill-mannered and ill-favoured in every way. Jade's life was changed for ever when she was picked out from her humble hovel to join a celebrated enclosed order of the time known as the Big Brothers.

Made up equally of men and women, the Brothers forsook all worldly goods and took a vow of celebrity, living communally in the "House" and dedicating their lives to ignorance and mutual abuse.

In a short while, Jade attracted a huge personal following, but alas she fell from grace when she unwisely addressed a comely young novice from the Indies as a "f****** Paki".

Poor Jade was expelled from the Big Brotherhood and was scorned and derided by the multitude.

Yet, in her misery and humiliation, Jade found grace. She earnestly repented and sought forgiveness from the Blessed Media.

Before long they relented, particularly when they discovered that she was dying.

Jade was now hailed throughout the land as a martyr and living saint. There was even a miracle, which astonished all those who witnessed it.

Jade had become betrothed to a young criminal of the time, by name Jack Tweed. But he was languishing in a prison cell.

Then lo, the gates of the prison were suddenly thrown open, thanks to the intercession of a well-known holy man of the time, St Jack of Straw.

The tags dropped from Tweed's leg and he walked free. And so it was that the couple were wed before the eyes of the nation, and Jade received a million gold coins from *Halo!* magazine.

Next week: St John of the Ross.

"The bird-feeder needs refilling, dear"

Those Secret Cabinet Minutes That JACK STRAW Won't Let Us Read – In Full

TOP SECRET
Minutes of Cabinet Meeting Held On 3 March, 2003

1. **Apologies**
Apologies for absence: R. Cook.

2. **Minutes**
The Minutes of the previous meetings were read by Mr A. Campbell and approved.

3. **Any Other Business**
The Prime Minister (A. Blair) announced that the President of the United States had decided to invade Iraq as soon as possible, and had also decided that Britain would join with him in the invasion.

The Prime Minister said that he was 100 percent behind the President on this matter, and asked Mr Campbell to hand round copies of a dossier he had prepared, in conjunction with the Joint Intelligence and Security Committee, proving why the need for the invasion was, in Mr Campbell's words, a "fucking no-brainer".

The Attorney-General (Mr Goldsmith) said that, since the previous meeting when he had expressed some reservations about the legality of invading a country for no reason at all, he had consulted a higher authority (Mr Blair) and was now "of a mind to support the Prime Minister in whatever it was that he and Mr Bush wished quite legally to do".

The Foreign Secretary (Mr Straw) said that he was sure he spoke for all his colleagues in congratulating the Prime Minister on his proposed course of action, and thanked him for letting the Cabinet know about the decision before it got in the papers.

The Prime Minister thanked Mr Straw for his loyal support, and asked the Chancellor (Mr Brown) whether his grumpy silence during the meeting could be taken as wholehearted support.

Mr Brown made a noise which was interpreted as "Yes".

Mr Blair then asked the Cabinet to demonstrate their backing for his proposed invasion with a show of hands.

Mr Campbell then explained to various ministers, including the Secretary of State for International Development (Mrs C. Short) that he knew where they lived, after which the motion was passed unanimously.

The Prime Minister closed the meeting by leading the Cabinet in a short chorus of his own composition, the words of which were as follows: "Forward, forward, never back, God's told me to invade Iraq".

There being no further business, it was decided to inform Mr Bush that his invasion could proceed as planned, and the meeting was closed.

DRAWING ALL FAITHS TOGETHER

A Letter From Our Founder And Spiritual Leader, the Rev. Imam Rabbi Sri Tony Blair

Hi!

As you may have seen, I was deeply honoured and privileged to be invited to President Obama's inaugural prayer breakfast at the White House in Washington.

Just imagine, a former vicar of St Albion's parish here in England being the very first world spiritual leader to be called to eat waffles and say "Hallelujah" at the table of the Rev. Martin Luther Obama.

And given this opportunity to preach the word, what was to be my message to this awesomely distinguished gathering including Sister Oprah Winfrey, Mr Waldo Walmart and Mr Snoop Doggy Dog (check names, please!).

The chief thing I had to tell my very old friend Brother Barack was how important it is for a politician to make clear at all times that he is acting under the guidance of Almighty God.

In all my years running my little parish in England (before my mission went "global"!), I always insisted to those around me in the vicarage how vital it was to "do God".

I well remember one of our parish team, Mr Campbell, who used to edit our parish newsletter, saying to me, "Vicar, watch it, you scumbag, or people will think you're a f***ing lunatic".

How wrong he was! If anyone was a f***ing lunatic, it was him, as numerous psychiatrists could testify!

But, as I said at our historic prayer breakfast in Washington, as I passed a plate of hominy grits to the lovely Michelle, "You must have God on your side in everything that you do".

This means that, when it all goes wrong, you can blame God – not that it did ever go wrong in my case, because everything I did was right.

Michelle then asked me what I thought about her husband's predecessor, the Rev. Dubya of the Church of the Latter-Day Morons.

I had to confess that I didn't know who she was talking about – and when I had repeated this three times, a nearby rooster crowed a resounding cock-a-doodle-doo. A good omen, surely.

When I had completed my address, which the congregation apparently found "deeply inspiring" (so much so that many of them broke off open-mouthed from their plates of hash browns and "sunny-side up" eggs to listen), Brother Obama thanked me for my witness, saying, "Praise the Lord, for a great prophet has come among us, to preach the message of Daft-ism to all the nations.

"Rev. Blair, you have set a shining example of moral leadership which us humble mortals can only hope to follow."

I don't mind admitting that I was very moved by this unsolicited testimonial from the world's most popular and powerful human being.

And, at this point, I pulled out my trusty guitar and sang a chorus which I had composed specially for the occasion.

"There's nothing odd, odd, odd, About doing God, God, God. We're all in his squad, squad, squad, So give him a nod, nod, nod, And put this song on your iPod, Pod, Pod."

I am happy to say that there were many people in tears by the time I had finished, and more than one of them was generous enough to approach me afterwards to say, "If only you were our President and spiritual leader, how much happier we would be."

I could only agree with their kind words.

Rev. T. Blair

Chief Executive, D.A.F.T.
(former vicar of St. Albion's)

Nursery Times

Friday, February 20, 2009

'WE'VE DONE A GOOD JOB' CLAIMS DUKE OF YORK

by Our Military Staff **General Retreat**

THE Commander of British forces in Operation Hill told the *Nursery Times* today that everyone could be proud of what his men had achieved in their recent deployment on the hill.

"The effort required in reaching the top of the hill was considerable but well worth it in terms of what we have achieved. We leave the hill in much better condition than we found it."

On other pages
● Cow Collides With Satellite Dish in Moon Jump **2**
● Eggs Not Good For You Says Humpty's Wall **3**
● Golliwog Loses Job **94**

"See? 'Tis a national treasure map"

POLICE LOG

Neasden Central Police Station

0815 hrs All officers were required to attend the Video Surveillance Room, to study CCTV footage compiled the previous evening in assorted local public houses. These included the Bee And Drainpipe (formerly the Duke Of Cambridge), the Wallis And Vomit (formerly the Queen Victoria) and the Laptop And Lapdancer (formerly the Boston Arms). Officers identified 25 possible criminal actions being committed, including sexual harassment, use of language likely to incite racial hatred, singing without a music licence, unauthorised gambling (i.e. dominoes), excessive consumption of alcohol (i.e. 2 units for men, 1.5 for women, 1.75 for members of transgender community) and, worst of all, several flagrant acts of smoking in a workplace.

0832 hrs Session suspended due to emergency call-out to apprehend elderly female suspect who was the subject of a formal complaint by Mr Darren Yobb, 16, a self-employed graffiti artist. While attempting an act of vandalism on the local war memorial, Mr Yobb was savagely assaulted by Mrs Ethel Prunehat, who was armed with a dangerous weapon, viz a rolled up copy of Good News, the parish magazine of the combined nearby churches of St Ivel and St Bruno. Twenty-four officers supported the station's Armed Response Unit in successfully apprehending Mrs Prunehat with a 50,000-volt taser device, thus incapacitating her and preventing her from inflicting further injury on the complainant. The suspect was taken to the Neasden Mortuary for questioning, whilst Mr Yobb was offered counselling by the Victim Support Unit.

1200 hrs All officers reported for the Divisional Poker Tournament. This initiative is designed to promote institutional bonding between officers of all ranks. Regrettably, this left no one to man the station phone line, resulting in a number of members of the public claiming to have died because of a lack of police response to their pleas for help. A full internal inquiry has been launched into how these persons managed to obtain classified data (i.e. the station phone number).

> Do come along, dear. It's time for luncheon

THE BIBLICAL TIMES

CLIMATE CHANGE 'ALARMIST' ATTACKED

by Our Ecological Staff **Ferdinand Mount Ararat**

CLAIMS by leading environmentalist, Noah, that sea levels were going to rise dangerously and that an unprecedented increase in rainfall would create a flood that would engulf the entire world, were dismissed yesterday as "alarmist nonsense".

Noah's Barking

At a conference of leading flood deniers in the Holy Land, one speaker, Professor Rainstorm, claimed, "It is not uncommon at this time of year to see 96 inches of rain fall in an hour or to see certain animal species going two-by-two aboard arks and glug... glug... glug..."

ON OTHER PAGES

● Your Rains Tonight

"What?"

From The Message Boards

Police are servants not masters says watchdog

u cant get the servant's these days! lol – *Danny_Daz*

Police state? Yes, and one to be proud of! The test of a true democracy is the freedom to police, and Britain is a world class democracy with a robust police service built for purpose. As a Labour Party member I am disappointed by the unhelpful attitude of the opposition parties. If only they and their friends in the media displayed a fraction of the commitment and enthusiasm shown by the police. – *Ros_Beeney*

comisioner of the met shuld of told brown the clown "NOT" on my beat sun-shine u go an meet ur g20 mate's in some1 elses country 😠 – *Bankrupt_Britan*

its bash a bobby time again 🌀 intresting that not one person complaning about the police made a citizans arest of an officer – *Think_about_it*

Being ex-job myself I am dismayed by the behaviour of the police. In my day we dealt with mobs like that in a couple of minutes – and when we hit them they stayed hit. ☺ Someone at Scotland Yard should bang a few heads together. – *Brian*

i was there and i saw the police attack the crazy penis guy who goes on all the demos, he started shouting some made up language, probably brain damaged – *1_World*

Thank you for your concern One World, but the language was Latin and my costume, as I explained recently in court, is not a penis. It is a giant finger, symbolising the wagging finger of the nanny state. On this occasion, however, it played an accusatory role, pointing the finger of blame at the financiers who have ruined our country. Unfortunately, during one "pointing" gesture I toppled over and accidentally broke a window at the Royal Bank of Scotland. This gave the police the perfect excuse to rough me up and confiscate my pamphlets. (These explain the connection between Gordon Brown, Sir Fred Goodwin, Barack Obama, Baroness Young and Osama Bin Laden.) – *Edwin*

edwin can u rep 4 us in norf weezy bruv? – *Zaks_bak*

Time to end the disastrous democratic experiment. – *Sword_of_Truth*

1984

(updated 2009 edition)

... On each landing, opposite the lift-shaft, the poster with the enormous face gazed from the wall. It was one of those pictures which are so contrived that the eyes follow you about when you move. GOOGLE IS WATCHING YOU, the caption beneath it ran.

Inside the flat a fruity voice was extolling the virtues of Google's new 'Street View' service. The voice came from the 'Google Screen', an oblong metal plaque like a dulled mirror which formed part of the surface of the right-hand wall. On the Google screen Winston could see a crystal-clear image of his flat. "Bloody hell, I left the window open," said Winston, rushing to close it. Winston turned a switch and the voice sank somewhat, though the words were still distinguishable. Google could be dimmed, but there was no way of shutting it off completely... *(Cont. p. 94)*

The Queen Mum You'll Never See

by Our Art Correspondent **Baz Relief**

PRIVATE EYE can exclusively reveal the incredible story of "censorship from the top" which has denied the British public the right to see the late Queen Mother as she really was.

The behind the scenes row has come to light following the unveiling of a new 240-foot bronze statue of the widowed Queen Consort advertising her favourite tipple, "White Horse" whisky, which now stands on a hill overlooking Dover *(Surely in the Mall, London? Ed.)*.

The sculptor, Phil Plinth, 76, originally planned a series of 60-foot bas reliefs, showing the Queen Mother in a series of domesticscenes.

In one she is seen writing out a betting slip for the 3.30 at Uttoxeter. In another she is shown seated, watching the race on television, while her faithful retainer "Backstairs Billy" pours her a glass of Dubonnet. In a third she is seen in bed counting her winnings, as she tucks into a box of chocolates.

However none of these endearing scenes will be seen on the finished statue, as they were cruelly vetoed by *(cont. p. 94)*

"Can you hear me now?"

Oscars Frocks Shocks!

IT'S Oscar Time... and yet again our fashion editor **CAT HARPIE** gives out her gongs to the greatest gowns – and her razzies to the red carpet ragbags!

It's the Pitts! **Angelina** looks like she's raided a tomb for this drab black number! It's all gone from Brad to worse!

This beautiful under-stated gown is a great look for **Ms Jolie** to adopt! We wouldn't change(ling) a thing!

Penelope is sure to make all the guys "hola" with delight in this stunning gown! There are no (Spanish) flies on Ms Cruz!

This fussy number is Woody terrible! What a **"Cruz"**ing disappointment! If she dresses like this she'll end up a (Barcel) loner!

Oh no! What does **Rubina** think she's wearing?! It's **Ali** wrong! This isn't a kids' **Qureshi**, you know! Slum mistake surely!

What a slumdog's dinner of a dress! Where's the designer gown and the jewellery? **Rubina** doesn't look like a millionaire. *(You're fired, you silly bitch. Ed.)*

GOVERNMENT TO INTRODUCE 'QUANTITATIVE SLEAZING'

by our Parliamentary Staff **Phil Expense-Account**

THE PRIME Minister, Gordon Brown, yesterday controversially promised to dramatically increase the amount of sleaze in circulation in Britain.

He explained, "We need a massive injection of sleaze to help the public lose confidence in this government."

He then detailed his five-point plan to bring the country to its knees.

1. Government ministers to claim porn films on expenses.

2. Government ministers to claim caravans as primary residences.

3. Government ministers to pretend to be living with their parents to claim allowances.

4. Government ministers to pretend to be living with their sisters to claim allowances.

5. Government MPs to participate in steamy Westminster love romps with mistresses in black stockings and suspenders. Cor! Phew! *(That's enough five-point plan, Ed)*.

The Prime Minister said he was confident that this introduction of "quantitative sleazing" would take the country back to the golden period of the last days of John Major's government.

"Henry, this keeping up with the Joneses is getting tiresome"

Can we claim that with the sink?

You lot are a complete shower

G20 – BROWN PROMISES NEW STABLE DOOR

by Our Economics Staff in Horse-sham, West Sussex

THE Prime Minister last night pledged that at the forthcoming International Summit in London all the world leaders would sign up to his plan to mend the stable door.

Said the Prime Minister, "We cannot ignore the fact that the horse may have already done a certain amount of bolting, but future generations will not forgive us if we do not institute the necessary measures to instigate a new door security regime process.

"Plans are already advanced,"

he said, "to install a new-look door with all the latest safeguards to prevent it ever opening again.

Gee-Gee 20

"State-of-the-art hinges are to be put in place with an international fail-safe locking mechanism, which all the countries in the world have already agreed to."

However, when asked if he had any idea where the horse was or how they could get it back into the stable, Mr Brown was unavailable for comment.

'BROWN SHOOTS SPOTTED' Claims Chancellor

by Our Recession Staff **Phil Job-Centres**

ALISTAIR Darling last night gave the clearest signal yet that the recovery is "far from under way".

He told MPs that he had "definite evidence of sightings of Brown Shoots".

"Believe me," he told the House of Commons, "it is not all doom and gloom out there. It's much worse. Everywhere I look, things are withering and dying. That is what I call Brown Shoots."

LATE NEWS

■ Brown Shoots Darling

G20 – How The World Saw Gordon's Triumph!

TOMLINSON: NEW FOOTAGE

He says he lives down this street

Not for long

THE POLICE
An Apology

IN COMMON with all other newspapers, we may have given the impression that during the recent demonstrations in central London, Mr Ian Tomlinson, a news vendor, died of a heart attack and was immediately attended by sympathetic police officers, who bravely attempted to resuscitate him while being bombarded with a hail of bottles, bricks and other missiles thrown by a mob of anarchists.

Headlines such as "Our brave boys in blue battle to save dying man from rioters", "Heartless anarchists hinder Met Samaritans" and "String up these murderous leftie scum" may have led readers to believe that the part played by the Metropolitan Police in the events surrounding the death of Mr Tomlinson was in some way commendable.

We now realise, having examined photographic evidence of the incident sent in by our readers, that there was not a jot nor scintilla of truth in any of the above. We are happy to accept that Mr Tomlinson was attacked from behind by an officer of the Metropolitan Police, wielding a baton, and was left to die on the roadside, comforted only by concerned members of the anarchist community. We would like to apologise for any distress or confusion caused by our credulity and laziness and our desire to cover our pages with pictures of Michelle Obama, rather than find out what's going on.

NEWS VENDOR WAS 'TOP TERRORIST SUSPECT'
Knacker's Shock Claim

by Our Crime Team **Troilus** and **Cressida Dick**

CHIEF Inspector 'Knacker of the Yard' Knacker last night lashed out at critics of the police, who had suggested that the police had somehow gone "over the top" in their treatment of the late newspaper seller Mr Juan Carlos de Tomlinson.

"Obviously it is a tragic shame that Mr Tomlinson died shortly after being assaulted by one of my team, Officer Z," said the Inspector, "but we were in a highly dangerous riot situation and we had every reason to suppose that Mr de Tomlinson was a known terrorist who was about to blow himself up, along with most of London.

"We have examined the CCTV footage very carefully," said Knacker, "and it is quite clear that officers issued Mr de Tomlinson with a clear warning, even though there is no sound on the footage.

"Highly-trained Scotland Yard lipreaders," he went on, "have confimed that shortly before Mr de Tomlinson's unfortunate demise, Officer Z shouted 'Stop! Proceed no further. I am an armed police officer, using my powers under the Prevention of Terrorism and Anything We Don't Approve Of Act 2006 to assist you in falling to the ground'.

"Mr Tomlinson ignored this very reasonable request," Knacker concluded, "and, sadly, the rest is history."

Officer Z has been commended for his "bravery" and has been promoted to become Sergeant Y.

'POPE OUT OF TOUCH WITH CATHOLICS,' Says Blair

by Our Religious Affairs Correspondent
Christopher Howseyourholyfather

THE LEADER of the world's two billion Roman Catholics, Tony Blair, today issued an encyclical, De Benedicto Geriatrico Homophobico, pointing out that the Pope "has little idea what ordinary Catholics like myself think about the big issues of the, you know, day."

Hail Blairy

Interviewed in the magazine *Platitude* by the leading gay mystic, Johann Hari Krishna, Mr Blair, a former Anglican clergyman, said, "I have been a Catholic for at least five minutes, and I think I am well qualified to tell the Pope what to do.

"Frankly, he's old and past it, and it's time for a new leader to take over, someone more in touch with the world as it is."

Full of shit

"Hey, let's get real about this," continued Father Blair. "We need a new Catholicism, providing a new People's Religion for all the millions of people out there who are looking for a charismatic, new spiritual leader who doesn't believe in all that old Catholic rubbish."

That Honorary Degree Citation In Full

SALUTAMUS FREDUS GOODWINUS APPELLATUS "FREDUS SHREDDUS" QUONDAM IMPERATOR BANKI ROYALIS CALEDONIAE ET NATWESTUM COUTTSQUE ET PRIMUS ADVISOR GORDONI BRUNIS IN REBUS ECONOMICIS ET FINANCIALES FAMOSISSIMUS PER INCOMPETENCIA ASTRONOMICA ET CUPIDITAS INCORRIGIBILIA IN SCANDALO SUB-PRIMO TOXICUS ET RESPONSIBILIS PER MAXIMI LOSSI CORPORATI IN HISTORIA MUNDI (XXVIII BILLIONES LIBRA APPROXIMO) SED AMASSAVIT FORTUNAM PERSONALIAM GRANDISSIMAM INCLUDENS GIGANTICUM PENSIONEM (MMMMM ETC.) ET BONUS VASTUS (MMMMMM ETC.) ET REFUSAVIT REDONERE SINGULARIS DENARIUS AD PUBLICUM UNIVERSALITER ACCLAMATUS "TERRIFICUS CROOKUS. STRINGIMUPUS" GAUDEAMUS, SIR FREDUS!

PRICES SOAR AS DEFLATION KICKS IN

by Our Economic Staff **Anatole Katastrophsky**

AS I predicted only yesterday, the nightmare of inflation has been succeeded by the spectre of deflation.

Which is which? This is the question which is puzzling some of the world's greatest economists, including myself.

The answer is simple. Inflation is when prices are rising by 3 percent.

And deflation is the same.

Good night. Could I have my cheque, please?

© *Timeswillgetworse Productions 2009.*

Gandalf   **Peaches Gandalf**

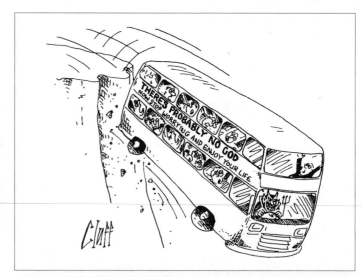

THAT SECRET ANTI-TERROR DOCUMENT NOTE IN FULL

THE EYE can reveal for the first time the uncensored briefing note that put an end to the career of high-flying Assistant Commissioner Bob Thick.

Phone dentist. **TOP SECRET**

Important: Whatever happens, do not be photographed getting out of a car holding this. Put in a file underneath some other papers, so it will not be seen.

Operation: Cockup

Procedure: Dawn swoop on the following terrorist suspects:

1. Mr O. bin Laden, Flat C, The Peabody Estate, Hattersley Road, Edgbaston.
2. Mr al Qaeda, Flat B, The Peabody Estate, Hattersley Road, Edgbaston.
3. The Late Mr Saddam Hussein, Flat A, The Peabody Estate, Hattersley Road, Edgbaston. *Pick up Dry cleaning*

● Numbers of officers required: 1,999

● Force level: Maximum

● Fire power: Assault rifles, machine guns, tanks and strategic nuclear weapons in case of dirty bomb.

Starting this week... an exciting new column by

STANLEY JOHNSON

(Father of Boris Johnson, Mayor of London)

What ho, readers! It's Boris's dad here! Johnson senior, as it were. And let me make two things clear straightaway. One, I haven't been given this job because I'm Boris's pater. And, two, I am completely different from Boris in every way. Comprenez? Cripes, blimey. I've had a very interesting career in my own right, and you can read all about it in my new book, "I Was Boris's Dad"!

Toodle pip!

Stanley

A review of Stanley Johnson's book by Rachel Johnson appears on p. 94

A review of Stanley Johnson's book by Rachel Johnson appears on p. 94

Is This The Face Of Shakespeare?

A SENIOR BBC executive has made an astonishing discovery of a new portrait of "the greatest artistic genius in the history of the world".

With his trim beard and penetrating gaze, it seems likely that this is the famous "Beard of Avon" rather than, as experts previously thought, the Regional Head of Paperclips at BBC North.

But some critics dismiss the new portrait as unconvincing. "How anyone could mistake this nonentity Shakespeare for the amazing and brilliant Alan Botney is a mystery. This is the man who has given the world such masterpieces as *"Midsummer Night's Repeat"* and *"As You Don't Like It"*.

"Tsk... Come on!"

From The Message Boards

Members of the online community respond to the major issues of the day...

Romanians driven from their Belfast homes

i studded this issue at uni and its a deep seeded problem. dur-ing the 19'60s there were violent programme's in Northern Island and the protestent's burned the romanian catholic's out of there home's. learn from history ppl! – *Jace_91*

The Romanians of South Belfast did no more than flee to their own land. Inasmuch and insofar as they did so do, then, as Isaiah taught, they did no more than the chased roe and the sheep that no man taketh up. – *Mr_Salmon*

not bein funy but y r they driv-ing them from there home's and who pay's 4 the driver's?– *Hayley_321*

pikey's mugg-ing off the uk taxpayer again 😡 MAKE THEM WALK!!!! 😡😡😡 – *Credit_Crunchie*

Gipsies set up camp near Tessa Jowell's house last year. Let's escort this lot to her second home. – *Cyril_ the_cynic*

Now there's a "gypsy awareness month" in the Midlands. Particularly pointless given that they raise awareness of themselves so effectively with their noise, rubbish, thieving and threats. – *Brown_out*

Romanians and gypsies are heavy smokers, and my children are terribly sensitive to any air pollution. I know this particular gang are returning to their own country, but I worry that others might move to England and exploit our tolerant nature. My youngest daughter now has nightmares about smoky caravans in our garden. – *Emily*

Any smoking gippsys come near my girls I swear Ill do time – *Family_ Man*

Let's all get together, protestant, catholic, Romanian and ordinary person alike. Let's suck our Murray mints and cheer Andy to victory! – *Murray_Maniac*

I'm wearing lucky pants for Andy! 😊 I haven't changed them since May and he hasn't lost a match! – *Bomber_ Lancaster*

Come ON Tim! – *Where's_Your_ Henman_Hat?*

Great stuff guys! – *Bogbrush*

TESCO OF THE D'URBERVILLES

GUIDE TO DORSET

Yes, It's The Poppadom Proms!

by Our Arts Correspondent
Sir Henry Bollywood

FOR the first time ever, the Albert Hall will pulsate to the sound of the greatest Indian film music ever written whilst thousands of scantily clad Asian lovelies gyrate to the strains of Tchaikovsky's Nutcracker Suite *(Is this right? Ed)*.

Make no mistake! The Proms have gone spicy! Phew! Two pints of lager and a naan bread, please, Maestro!

18 July: What You Will Hear
Massala's 7th Symphony "The Slumdog", played by the Balti-more Symphony Orchestra of Mumbai conducted by Sir Daniel Baren-Boyle.

POLICE LOG

Neasden Central Police Station

0900 hrs Officers despatched to Ratner's Quality Jewellery Emporium in Costcutter Road to prevent major robbery by suspicious afro-caribbean suspect, observed looking in the window whilst armed with a dangerous crutch due to a fractured metatarsal.

Officers duly apprehended Neasden FC's Nigeria-born striker Moses Onanugu, 25. The suspect was handcuffed and found to be in possession of large sums of money (£20) which it transpired was his weekly salary from Neasden FC, with which he had intended to purchase a new watchstrap for his father in Lagos.

Onanugu was charged with Aggravated Window Shopping and Inciting Racial Hatred amongst police officers.

1200 hrs All officers to attend "Welcome Home Our Heroes March" by men of the North Circular Rifles returning from Basra.

1207 hrs All officers redeployed to provide protection for anti-March demonstrators from the Neasden branch of the Al Quaeda Support Association, leader Abu bin Asda, bearing placards, eg "Death to the Basra Murderers", "Slaughter the British Rapists" and "End Free Speech Now".

Following exchanges of abuse between demonstrators and bystanders, two of the troublemakers (ie the bystanders) were immediately taken into custody under the Prevention of Religious Hatred Act 2009.

1600 hrs The demonstrators finally dispersed under police escort to the North London Synagogue in order to commit acts of graffiti, arson, etc.

1800 hrs Officers commended for their heroic conduct during the march and plans made for a "Salute Our Brave Boys In Blue" Police victory parade from the tube station to the Star of Luton Curry House in Pricerite Road.

"He was very fond of his bees"

The Evidence Of SIR MAX MOSLEY To The Commons Culture Media And Sport Committee – Chairman, SIR JOHN WHIPPINGDALE MP

Whippingdale *(for it is he)*: It is very good of you, Sir Max, to give up some of your valuable time to answer our questions today.

Sir Max: As it happens, I am missing a very important engagement this afternoon in Mayfair.

Whippingdale: May we enquire what the nature of this engagement might have been?

Sir Smacks: It is a private matter.

Rosemary McCaner MP *(for it is she)*: You mean, you have not told your wife?

Sir Smacks: Precisely. Not that I am ashamed of what I would have been doing with Ms A, Ms B and Ms C. It is just that it is, as I say, a personal affair and of no concern to anyone else, least of all the pornographers of the News of the World.

Whippingdale: You mean these people, Sir Smacks?

(Holds up copy of News of the World with headline "F1 Boss In S&M Nazi Sex Orgy Shock")

Can you tell us how you felt when you saw this headline at your breakfast table?

Sir Smacks: It is impossible to describe how painful it was.

McCaner: I thought that is what you liked?!

Sir Smacks: Don't interrupt, schweinhund!

Whippingdale: We do apologise, Sir Smacks. I can see you are clearly distressed by the memory of this appalling revelation.

Sir Smacks: Imagine my feelings, ladies and gentlemen, after 45 years of being a respectable sado-masochist, suddenly to find my dignity is stripped away and I am dragged through the gutter.

McCaner: I thought that was the bit you liked!

Sir Smacks: I haf told you vonce before, Englischer pig dog... shut up or I vill be forced to haf you shot at dawn!

Whippingdale: I must apologise, Sir Whacks, and I speak for all the members of the committee when I assure you that you have our heartfelt sympathy. Clearly, the irresponsible and wicked press have overstepped the mark and must be brought into line before they start looking into the private lives of all of us. Not that I have anything to hide, I hasten to add, and I think I speak again here for all members of the whole House.

All: Hear, hear! Good old Sir Whacks!

Whippingdale: So may we conclude this enquiry by congratulating you, Sir Whacks, on your brave campaign to ensure that all journalists in Europe who have ever written about you are locked up in a dark dungeon with German wardresses to keep them in order with suitable implements of correction.

McCaner: Hang on, isn't that what you enjoy?

Smacks: DUMBKOPF!!! (Screams). I am not ashamed or embarrassed in the least. Like my late father, I am only concerned with the freedom of every Englishman to be locked up in a dungeon for most of the war like he was.

Whippingdale: Spank you very much indeed.

One must adopt the local customs otherwise one will look silly

MY BATTLE WITH THE HELL OF ADDICTION

by Julie Myexson

At first it seemed innocent enough. Almost a laugh. Just experimenting to see what it was like. But all too soon it became a habit. And then a terrible addiction that would threaten to destroy my family. I just couldn't stop writing about my children.

It started with the odd piece in a newspaper. Then it got more regular, more and more pieces, then a column and then a book and then another one.

My family tried everything to stop me. Rows, threats, blackmail – none of it worked. They even changed the locks on my study but I smashed the door down and wrote even more articles.

Eventually there was no option but to try the "Tough Love" technique that American experts recommended. No matter how much I adored my computer (as only a writer can) I had to take the ultimate step and throw it out of the house. So I did.

But then, only five minutes later, I relented, ran into the street, pulled it out of the gutter and brought it back inside, hoping that this time I wouldn't relapse and just write yet another piece about my family.

But I did. And here it is. Will this do?

THE DAILY TELEGRAPH   Friday, April 3, 2009

An Open Letter To JULIE MYERSON
From Polly Filler

Dear Julie,

We've been friends for years, but I have to tell you frankly, Julie – this time you've gone way too far. Yes, you're a writer like me. Yes, we all need to make a living. But Julie, no... you mustn't exploit your family simply to fill up those column inches. I know it's hard, but as I said to my toddler Charlie when he was asked to leave St Duncestan's for setting fire to the class hamster, "Don't worry, darling, I would never write about you and embarrass you in public just because you've done something funny." And you know what? He took off his shorts and showed everyone in Caffè Nero his little pink bottom! Bless!!

Later, I asked my partner Simon what he thought about your behaviour, Julie, and whether he thought you had betrayed your loved ones. And you know what he said? Nothing. He just lay there uselessly in front of the TV, drinking lager, smoking dope and giggling inanely at *Heston Blumenthal's Extreme Vomiting* on Channel More Four Plus Four Extra!!

So, I'm sorry, Julie. The Filler Jury is against you. I, and I suspect millions of others like me, won't be buying your book. Instead they'll all be buying *"Take The Mummy and Run – A True Life Account of Polly Filler's Ghastly Family!"* (£19.99 Johnson, Johnson and Johnson Books).

With love,
Polly.

Letters *to the* Editor

The Real Stalag Luft 3

SIR – The recent reunion of the veterans of Stalag Luft 3 has rightly focused yet again on the lamentable historical inaccuracies contained in the so-called film *The Great Escape*. Those of us who were there, as I was privileged to be, were to a man infuriated by this travesty of the facts.

For a start, the late Mr Steve McQueen was never an inmate of the camp, as portrayed by Hollywood. Furthermore, he did not possess a motorcycle capable of vaulting a six-foot barbed wire fence as he raced to freedom at the climax of the film.

Even more heinous is the scene showing a British officer addressing a crowd of other ranks as "you lot" – a vulgar expression which only came in in the 1950s. He would, of course, have addressed them as "you chaps". This anachronism exemplifies the complete lack of any proper historical research.

As for the tunnels, the idea that they were called "Tom", "Dick" and "Harry" is patently balderdash. The three tunnels, as I can vouch, were known respectively as "The M1", "The Hyde Park Underpass" and "Euro Tunnel".

For the record, it was to my eternal regret that I was unable to join those gallant comrades who took part in the subterranean escape. I was next on the list, but at the last minute I was disqualified by the Camp's acting medical officer on the grounds that I had been incapacitated due to over-indulgence in the excellent spirit distilled from local beetroots and acorns which was regularly served at meetings of the Escape Committee. I was deemed UFT (unfit for tunnel) and my place was taken by my old friend Squadron-Leader Frobisher, who, dressed as a nun, managed to reach the "safe haven" of Bruges, where an RAF light bomber was sent in to rescue him. But that is another film!

Wing-Commander Herbert Gussett UFT
The Old Hangover, Luft St. Alag, Dorset

"Oh, he's my muse"

TV Highlights

BBC1	8.00pm	**Gavin and Stacey**
BBC2	9.00pm	**Horne and Corden**
BBC3	9.30pm	**Gavin and Corden**
BBC4	10.00pm	**Horne and Stacey**
BBC1	10.30pm	**Jonathan Ross with Gavin and Stacey's Horne and Corden**
BBC2	11.00pm	**Graham Norton with Horne and Corden's Gavin and Stacey**
BBC3	11.30pm	**Corden and Corden**
BBC4	12.00am	**Horne and Horne**

(That's enough Horne and Corden, Ed.)

Radio Highlights

BBC7	**Round the Horne and Corden**

(I said, that's enough. Ed)

Film Highlights

Shaun of the Dead Similar Lesbian Vampire Killers with TV's Corden and *(I really mean it, you're fired. Ed)*

POETRY CORNER

In Memoriam Simon Dee, Star of TV's 'Dee Time' and Old Salopian

So. Farewell
Then Simon
Dee.

You were
The quintessential
Sixties figure,
DJ and Chat show host.

Your real
Name, however,
Was Cyril Nicholas
Henty-Dodd.

"Henty-Dodd Time"
No, it
Does not
Sound the
Same.

> D.J. Thribb (17½)

In Memoriam: Sunny von Bülow

So. Farewell
Then Sunny von
Bülow.

American heiress
And suspected
Murder victim.

You were played
In the film
By Glenn Close.

And now
Your life has
Drawn to one.

> Klaus von Thribb (17½
> years, overturned on appeal)

In Memoriam Michael Crichton, Best-Selling Science Fiction Author

So. Farewell
Then Michael
Crichton.

Creator of
Jurassic Park,
In which dinosaurs
Were brought
Back to life.

In a million years' time
Will you be
Brought back
In similar fashion?

This is not
A question a
Poet can
Easily answer.

> E.J. Thribb (17½million years old)

POETRY CORNER

In Memoriam Kathy Staff, actress.

So. Farewell
Then Kathy Staff.
Better known as
Nora Batty
From *Last
Of The Summer
Wine*.
You were one of the
original cast.

Were you the
Last of the
*Last Of The
Summer Wine*?

Or is there still
Someone alive who I've
Forgotten?

I had this
Problem with my
Famous elegy for
Charles Bronson,
When I could not
Remember which of
The Magnificent
Seven were still
With us.

All together now –
Dum di-da-da-dum
Dum di-da-da-dum
Da-da
Di-da-DA-da...

> E.J. Thribb (Magnificent 17½)

**Lines On The Appointment Of
Mr Bear Grylls As Chief Scout**

So. Congratulations to
Bear Grylls.

You are the new
Chief Scout.

Yes, we have
Seen you on
TV.

An inspiration to
All Boy and
Girl Scouts.

You can show
Them how to
Survive by cooking
Spiders, snakes or voles.

If they survive
Long enough
They could even
Grill bears.

> E.J. Thribb (Poetry Proficiency Badge,
> Tooting & Balham 'Wolverine' Pack)

THE Sun

Friday, April 3, 2009

JADE GOODY STILL DEAD

IN an incredible new twist to her roller-coaster story *(cont. inside)*

SHOW US YOUR GRIEF, MA'AM!

Fury Builds As Queen Fails To Honour Jade

by Our Entire Staff

It's business as usual for Her Heartless Majesty

THERE was growing outrage last night as the Queen maintained her week-long silence over the death of Jade Goody.

Many of the world's leading figures have already paid their respects to the reality TV superstar, from Gordon Brown and David Cameron to Sir Stephen Fry himself, who went out of his way to issue a personal statement via Twitter.

Respect

But, as the entire nation united in grief, from Buckingham Palace there has been nothing but a resounding silence.

In former times, the passing of a national figure of Ms Goody's stature would have been marked by the monarch with a month of court mourning.

Palace officials would have been expected to wear black.

All Royal engagements would have been cancelled.

And the flag over the Palace would have been lowered to half-mast.

Grief

Yet, what has happened? With chilling insensitivity to the feelings of the people, the Queen has carried on her official business as if nothing had happened.

Not only did she receive the Governor of the Bank of England, but she was seen laughing and joking at a race meeting in Uttoxeter.

Said one angry mourner, Ms Denise Wetherspoon, a 25-year-old mother of three, as she queued to place her floral tribute on the mountain of flowers outside Ms Goody's home, "the Queen should be made to come out on that balcony and forced to cry in front of the entire nation. It's the least she could do to pay her respects."

Police chiefs warned of possible "civil disorder" and even a possible "nuclear outrage" if the Queen continues to flout public opinion and *(cont. p. 94)*

ON OTHER PAGES

Sun writers ask:

● Why isn't there a state funeral for Jade? **2**

● Come on, Elton – give us "Goody in The Wind" **3**

● Where are the plans for the Jade

Memorial Gardens? 4

● Should Good Friday become Goody Friday? **7**

● Did the Duke of Edinburgh murder Jade? asks Mohamed al Fayed

(That's enough. Ed.)

From Gnome Souvenirs

PRINCESS JADE 1981-2009

THE JADE GOODY MEMORIAL PLATE

THIS MOVING tribute to one of Britain's greatest heroines is now available in a limited edition of only 6 million. Handcrafted from green Jade-style porcelain in the Hong Kong workshops of oriental master craftsman Chee Po Tat, this unique plate is not only a historic souvenir, but is also an investment which in years to come will be treasured by your children and their children's partners' step-children and the people next door.

Although designed as an ornamental artefact, the Goody Plate can be used as a receptacle for burgers, fries, beans and similar nutritional items.

WARNING: Do not put the Goody Plate in the dishwasher, as the high temperatures may damage the green colouring, thus reducing the value of your priceless heirloom.

FURTHER WARNING: In some extreme instances the Goody Plate may, after exposure to hot water and detergent, reveal the image of the late Princess Diana with the legend "Diana the People's Princess 1961-1997". Gnome Limited Edition Artefacts accepts no responsibility for the above.

Yours for only £299.99 (+ VAT + p&p).
Send cash now to: Jade Goody Plate Offer, Unit 94, The Max Clifford Industrial Estate, Yeovil.

PC SALES

"I'm looking for something to help me waste time more efficiently"

58

NATION PLEADS TO SAVE CAINE
'Don't Go, Sir Michael'
Thousands of Protestors March on Downing Street

by Our Budget Staff **Sue Pettax**

A TEAR-stained Joanna Lumley led nationwide protests yesterday, calling on the government to reverse their "shameful treatment" of Sir Michael Caine, who has threatened to leave Britain in disgust at Mr Darling's draconian tax measures.

Said Sir Michael, "I am 76 years old and I am still working every day whilst these layabouts are getting benefits. Not a lot of people know that – except for taxi drivers.

Caine Mutiny

"I have served this country faithfully through two world war films," he continued, "including *Five Days To Antwerp* and *Ice Station Limoges*, not to mention the 79th remake of *They Flew To Bruges Again*."

Get Carter Fuck

Sir Michael has, of course, made many other unforgettable and distinguished films, including the cold war thrillers *The Ludlum Memorandum Condundrum* and *The Quimby File*, as well as the mercenary epic *Wild Turkeys III* and the classic comedy thriller *The Cushy Job*. *(That's enough films. Ed.)*

Billion Dollar Drain

An all-night vigil was held outside the House of Commons, as Caine's fans fought with Tamil protestors and elderly Gurkhas to demand an immediate repeal of the tax laws that will save Sir Michael from his voluntary exile.

FEARS OF BRAIN DRAIN AS 50% TAX BITES

by Our City Staff **Claire Desk**

BRITAIN could lose some of its most gifted bankers, experts warned yesterday.

In what could be a disaster for the country, there could be a mass exodus of top city talent fleeing the punitive new 50p rate of tax introduced in the Budget.

Said one expert, "Are we mad? This country can ill afford to lose the people who have contributed most to the economic crisis. Do we really want to drive the likes of Sir Fred Goodwin into exile?"

"Come off it, Mr Brown," he said. "This will lead to the end of civilisation as we *(cont. p94)*

Old Jokes Revisited No.94

Britons flee 50% tax stunner

Brown To Appear On Songs of Praise

What You Will Hear

In The Bleak Midsummer
Crock of Ages
Kum-By-Election
Fight The Wrong Fight
The Pay Thou Gavest
The Lord Mandelson Is My Shepherd
When I Survey The Wondrous Mess
Now Thank We All Our Gord
Everything Has Broken
I Vow Not To Go To The Country
(That's enough hymns, God)

That Budget Breakfast In Full

Freshly Squeezed Pips

– ❋ –

Choice of Cereal:
Fred the Shreddies, Credit Crunchy Nuts,
Money Nut Loopies, Cheerios

– ❋ –

Egg on Face
Hash Browns (with pinch of salt)
Waffles

– ❋ –

Choice of Teas:
Earl Very Grey, Alistair Darjeeling
English Breakfast, Scottish Dogs Dinner

"Do you ever feel we on the Left have drifted slightly from our aims when we first came to power?"

DIARY

KARL LAGERFELD

If you want to wear a headband, you must commit suicide immediately. But I beg you do not put a headband on before you do yourself away with, hm? To be seen dead in a headband is such a bore.

I'm mad for the economic downturn! Mad for it! Mass unemployment is so sexy, hm? When the economic graph swoops down like that, like a curve from Fragonard, I think it is so gorgeous, so trendy! My new evening wear range for Chanel is a wonderful homage to that curve, with all my clothes with downturns off the shoulders in dark, dark greys and delicious blacks.

They talk of green shoots of recovery! How disgusting! Green shoots are so ugly, so passé. When I see a green shoot in my garden, I have my gardener to get rid of it. "Dig it up and destroy it!" I tell him. I have no time for the Spring, it is the most vulgar and pretentious month. Hope and optimism? So Nineties. So démodé.

Karl's Top Five Tips for Surviving the Credit Crunch:

1. **Don't eat.** Eating is so Seventies and this is Today. I eat only celery and even that I am not enjoying. Pale green is so uninteresting.

2. **Dismiss your assistant chauffeur.** No-one has an assistant chauffeur any more. Assistant chauffeurs are so *yesterday*.

3. **You do not need more than 200 white shirts at any one time.** Anything more is excessive. I threw the rest of them away when I heard of the arrival of the credit crunch and I tell you I felt so *good* about myself!

4. **Forget charity.** Charity this, charity that. Tcha! I try to avoid charity. It is so *boring*, like tomato ketchup. I avoid charity. It doesn't happen for me. I'm rich enough not to have to do that. Thank God I don't have to do that. There are so many poor people who dress deplorably with no sense of style and they look so ugly and stupid and are always out begging. Do you want to encourage them, hm? Of course you do not! It would be different if they possessed any sense of *bravura*, if they styled themselves on the Ballet Russes, or they came out onto the streets with the Audrey Hepburn look. But they do not. The only charity that is acceptable is Save the Tiger, because at all costs we must not lose the real tiger fur, I just adore it, it is so *chic*.

The whale? Tcha! I would never save the whale. It is so *fat*, and who is to blame for that? The whale has let itself go, so it is not even size 18, it is something so much more, like size 35.

And why should I save the whale, when it has let itself go so ugly and morbidly obese? And all the *spouting* it does is so *horrible*. Imagine your reaction if I were to come in her spouting water out of my backside and into the air? I tell you this, you would not be offering me your chic charity money, and that is for sure.

5. **Never travel first-class.** It is so *common*. No-one should travel first-class, with all those strangers with their coughs and their germs. No: a private jet, or nothing at all.

I'm mad for books. I possess them everywhere in my houses. They are so chic. But too many of them in my opinion are about love. A man meets a woman. A man meets a man. They get on well. They become intimate. So what? It is all so *boring*.

So I am redesigning the books. I am being asked by the great House of Penguin to breathe the new life into their tedious back catalogue, to transform it by magic so it is less Seventies and so much more about *now* and *today*.

I tell them no more horrible romance, no ghastly touching if you please. Every morning, I awake early and I go into my studio and I take out my scissors to their catalogues and perform my magic.

Snip! Snip! Snip! This morning, I go to work on Lady Chatterley. Now we have Lady Chatterley, yes, but her lover is gone! Her tacky undressed lover has been disappeared by me and Lady Chatterley, she is back in a proper dinner-dress, with its fabulous lines, and no longer rolling around like a common size 14 in the mud but with good manners for once, I think.

The thing I hate most in life is when people come up to me and talk. I do not want a social life. I've had enough of it. Take it away from me. It's démodé, another era. In the 1990s, it was fashionable to talk to other people, but not now. Now, it is so uninteresting. They never have anything to say. Yesterday, an imbecile London cab driver he said to me, "Turned out nice again, guv." Of course, I refused to reply. Instead, I shut the chic little window between us. "Turned out nice again, guv": It's all so *boring*, hm?"

As told to CRAIG BROWN

THOSE NORTH KOREAN PIZZAS IN FULL

What you will now be able to eat in the pizzerias of Pyongyang

★ Tomato, Mozzarella and Sausage Dog

Tomato, Mozzarella and Hot Dog

Tomato, Mozzarella and Running D

Tomato, Mozzarella and Lap Dog

Anything you can't eat, take away in a doggy bag!!

TALES OF THE ANCIENT ROMANS

NO. XCIV BORUS JOHNSONIUS CINCINNATUS

IN THE early days of the Republic there lived a noble senator named Borus, respected for his oratory, erudition and his love romps with the beautiful nubian Princess Petronella.

The noble Borus won lasting fame when he drove the hated barbarian, Ken the Red, out of Londinium and established a golden era of peace and harmony in the capital. His work done, Borus retired to his smallholding in North Londinium and lived the life of a simple mayor, growing vegetables, cycling around the streets, drinking wine and surrounding himself with beautiful handmaidens.

The humble Borus had no ambition for higher office – except to be Prime Minister.

Said Borus to the adoring populace, "I will become your leader *only* if I am called – and even if I am not."

So saying, Borus rose from his labours, went down to the forum and stabbed his rival

Cameronus in the back.

"Et tu, Borus?" exclaimed the mortally wounded Cameronus.

"Crikeyus!" said Borus. "That was easier than I thought."

So Borus became dictator and soon declared himself a god.

Adapted from *The Decline and Fall of the British Empire* by Edward Gimson.

'Scottish Play' Opens

by Our Theatrical Staff Charles Edmund Spencer

MR WILLIAM Shagspaw's new tragedy, MacBroon, last night packed Ye Global Recession Theatre to its rafters (except that it hasn't got any).

As ye curtain rose, we saw a brooding Scottish psychopath planning to murder his country's leader Duncan Blair.

When he has finally steeled himself to commit the evil deed (after ten years of bitter soliloquising), MacBroon imagines that he will enjoy many years of power on the throne.

But, alas, a spectre intervenes at the feast. It is the Royal Banquo of Scotland, with a long line of other Banquos who have all perished in mysterious circumstances.

Everything goes wrong as MacBroon's kingdom falls apart. Finally, as has been foretold by the three witches (Hazel, Jacqui and Harriet), 'Andy Birnam Wood' comes to Anfield Stadium, where he is booed off the field.

MacBroon has now lost his wits, and pronounces "Is this a dagger I see in my back?"

In a final memorable speech he declares, "Tomorrow and tomorrow

and tomorrow, the recovery will begin."

But it is too late. Onto the stage springs the young Scottish laird Cameron McDuff, who lays claim to the crown, leaving MacBroon a corpse at his feet.

Many of last night's audience found Master Shockspure's new offering too depressing for words and advised him to stick to comedies such as 'Twelfth Nightclub' where Prince Harry is seen becoming inebriated at the Boujis Tavern (cont. p. 94)

BBC Radio 3

Opera Choice

Il Travestiati by Berlusconi

Act One of the famous *Opera Buffooni* opens with the Robber Baron holding one of his famous parties at the sumptuous Villa Pornograffi.

A chorus of semi-naked nymphs urge Silvio to turn up the central heating, singing the haunting aria *Tutti Titti Frizzi (Our Tiny Tits Are Frozen)*.

The festivities are then interrupted by two photographers, Papageno and Paparazzo, who hide in an olive tree in order to take pictures of the frolicking lovelies. The photographers sing *Millione et Tre (We're Going To make A Fortune From These Dirty Pix)*.

Act II The Robber Baron is furious and consults his lawyer, the elderly Pietro Cartero-Fucco, who advises

him to pass a privacy law at once, making it illegal to take pictures of the Robber Baron without his trousers *(Surely "consent"? Ed.)*.

Act III Silvio receives an unexpected visitor from England, Sir Maximilian Mosley, who tells him that he must punish the photographers for their intrusions into his private life, preferably by spanking them or whipping him dressed as a German officer.

Silvio laughs and the two of them sing the world-famous *Bums Sorus* from *Aieeeeeda!* *(That's enough Opera on 3. Ed.)*

Who are they – the wannabe winners of this year's Apprentice?

Kevin Twat, 23. Trouser-press Sales Executive, Swindon. Says: *"In my dictionary there's no word for second. Losing is for losers. It's winner takes the biscuit."*

Chantelle Byttche, 25. Nail Extension Entrepreneur, Solihull. Says: *"I don't take any prisoners. And if I do, I eat them for breakfast. 110%."*

Simon Aaze, 27. Phone Hygiene Manager, Croydon. Says: *"I shoot from the lip. I'm full-on, 24/7, 360 degrees of the year. Like it or lunch it."*

Sandra Kowe, 26. Paperclip Marketing Liaison Executive, Droitwich. Says: *"I'm not in this to make friends. I'm in it to make waves. And if people drown then that's the way the tough cookie crumbles."*

Colin Bollocks, 29. Ex-public School boy, Windsor. Says: *"Like, yah. Totally. Standard. I mean, let's do it. I'm fired."* (That's enough Apprentices, Ed.)

FRUMPY SCOT AMAZES WORLD

by Our Showbiz Staff
Phil Airtime

IT JUST shows how deceptive appearances can be. From the moment the dumpy, wild-haired Caledonian stomped onto the stage, the critics and audience were preparing to snigger and to jeer.

But what followed was little short of stunning.

The wannabe Prime Minister with the weird smile and the appalling dress sense suddenly opened his mouth and out came a sound that no one had expected.

It was the word "Sorry". We were all left aghast, feeling a mixture of shame and amazement.

Briton's Not Talent

How could we have misjudged the dour, dowdy 57-year-old Celt so badly?

How could we have laughed so smugly when the amateur from Fife shyly claimed that he would like to

be the next Tony Blair?

Yet, in the twinkling of an eye, the shy, never-been-loved-by-anyone Scot turned into an overnight political sensation.

"It was unbelievable," said one member of the audience, fighting back the tears. "You couldn't believe a word he was saying."

Gordon Is A Friend Of Moron

And now Gordon is hotly tipped to go all the way and lose the competition in spectacular fashion.

His entry has been posted on YouTube and has flashed around the world, receiving a remarkable total of no hits. Celebrities in Hollywood are not twittering about his extraordinary version of "sorry" and, to cap it all, he has not been invited on American TV's Oprah Winfrey show.

"It is like a fairytale come true," said one chastened critic. "A Grimm fairytale with a really unhappy ending where everyone dies and *(cont. p. 94)*

(cont. p. 94)

LITTLE BRITAIN

Pleased to meet you, Ma'am

Gosh, Dubya's caught the sun

"We've been invited to a black tie do – your mother has died, Neville"

TELEGRAPH HAS STORY SHOCK

Incredible Revelation Rocks Fleet Street

by Our Telegraph Staff **Mr Cheque** and **Mr Book**

THE WORLD of journalism was rocked to its foundations today when the Daily Telegraph ran a good story on its front page.

Gone were the familiar pictures of Kate Middleton and fruity girls getting their A Level results.

Instead, readers gasped at pictures of Phil Woolas and Michael Gove *(Who they? Ed.)* accompanied by detailed accounts of how MPs are fiddling their expenses.

Editor Will Lewis was forced to apologise, saying, "I am very sorry about what has happened. It is true that we paid a very large sum of money for this story, but we did not break any rules."

But not all Telegraph readers were impressed.

Said one, "It's a disgrace. I buy the Telegraph to collect vouchers for a two-for-one Eurostar City Break in beautiful Bruges – and all I get is some story about David Willetts and his light bulbs."

● **Full story and special Telegraph light bulb offer** 94

NEWSAGENT

"I want to cancel the Telegraph I've been claiming on expenses"

Nursery Times

Friday, May 29, 2009

NURSERYLAND'S OLDEST MOTHER

by **Hans Christian Democrat**

A 66 year old woman who lives in a shoe is expecting her first baby today but remains defiant in the face of criticism.

"I feel like a young woman," said the sexagenarian, "and I will probably have many more children. Possibly so many that I won't know what to do."

Social Services expressed their concern about the potential consequences of "old parenting", which they said could include unsuitable diets – broth, lack of bread, etc – and, in extreme cases,

How it might look

physical abuse such as whipping soundly and putting to bed.

On other pages
● Cat in Fiddle Shock – Calls for Resignation **2**
● "I will pay back stolen porridge," says Shamed Goldilocks **3**
● Crooked Man in Crooked House – "I Have Done Nothing Wrong" **94**

OBITUARY
Dany La Wolf

Forest mourns great female impersonator wolf who famously dressed up as Red Riding Hood's grand mother.

EXPENSES SCANDAL ■ DAY 94 ■

Exclusive to Private Eye after reading the Daily Telegraph

❶ SIR BUFTON TUFTON Conservative *(North Freebyshire, Scotland)* claimed £90,000 for returfing his croquet lawn at his second home in Market Barkworth, Wiltshire. Also invoiced £210,000 for bag of frozen carrots from Tesco. The Parliamentary Fees Office refused the carrots but allowed an electric toothbrush £17.94 for Sir Bufton's gamekeeper.

❷ PATSY JACKET Labour *(Swillett, East Staffs)* claimed £310,000 for holiday chalet in Southwold which she called her "primary secondary residence". Also claimed £1.95 for fly swat. The Fees Office refused a £2 million bill for an extension to Ms Jacket's property "to accommodate a private feepaying school for boarders between 13 and 18".

❸ JASPER TROUGH Tory *(Bucksbridge)* claimed £2 million for a new wallet "to put all his expenses in". Registered the wallet in the name of his civil partner Jason Beau-Gusse but was told by the Fees Office that the claim was unacceptable because it was "too small".

❹ BARBARA FLOGGETT Labour *(Grasping Under Hande, Notts)* claimed £750,000 for round-the-clock security to protect her from angry taxpayers who wanted to "set fire to her house and string her up for being an MP".

❺ SEAMUS O'SHAMELESS Sinn Fein *(Ballyclava, Antrim)* claimed £500,000 for second home in London which he said was necessary for him to fulfil his non-attendance commitment at the House of Commons.

(More names tomorrow and the next day and the one after that if the Telegraph is still running the story)

SECOND HOME SECRETARY LATEST

It's the Bill!

I'll put it on expenses

"Haven't you lot got second homes to go to?"

Teenage Boy 'Not His Own Father' Shock

IN AN extraordinary twist to the underage father saga that is being played out in the nation's tabloids, DNA tests have revealed that 13 month old Baby Alfie is NOT his own father.

The baby is said to be devastated, having previously entered the history books as the youngest parent of himself in Britain.

In fact, his father is a more conventional 15 month old boy from the same estate.

© *News of the Weird*

"Don't be silly... we've got our heels on"

POETRY CORNER

In Memoriam
The South Bank Show: LWT's Flagship Arts Programme 1978-2010

So. Farewell
Then *The South
Bank Show* and its
Famous compere
Lord Bragg of
Wigton.

You will be remembered
For such highlights
In the culture of
Our time as
George Michael smoking
Pot and
Francis Bacon
Getting drunk.

But most of all you
Will be missed for
Your immortal
"Catch tune"
by Julian Lord-Webber.

All together now.
Dum-diddy-diddy-diddy
Dum-dum-dum
Etc.

E.J. Thribb (17½)

This week's Opera Special – the new Garsington production of Berlusconi's hilarious comic opera *The Marriage of Silvio*

Act One
The Robber Baron, Silvio, has left his wife the Countess Veronica back in their castle, the Palazzo Sleazio, in order to attend the 18th birthday party of a beautiful peasant girl, the gorgeous Poutella.

He showers her with presents, including a priceless golden necklace. He sings to her the aria *'Zucchero Papa Voglio'* (*'Let Me Be Your Sugar Daddy'*).

She replies to him with the immortal *'Che Sera Sera'* (*'I Would Like To Be On One Of Your TV Stations'*).

Act Two sees the arrival of the unhappy Veronica who, spying the couple together, flies into a rage. She cries out *'Lothario bastardo'* and then sings the classic *'Nessun Dorma'* (*'You'll Never Sleep With Me Again'*).

Silvio replies to her angry accusations by singing *'No Sono Paedophilio'* (*'She Was 18 And I checked'*). The Act ends with him calling for his lawyers.

Act Three opens with the arrival of the comic legal duo, Carteri and Fucco, who advise the furious Baron that he should sue his wife for defamation (*'Scandalo Magnato'*).

Veronica has meanwhile called *her* own lawyer, Antonio Julio Caersar, who tells her that she will get half his fortune (*'Billione e Tre'*).

As the couple and their respective lawyers are shouting and arguing, there is a clap of thunder and suddenly the terrifying figure of the Pope appears in their midst and drags Silvio down to hell. *(Is this right? Ed.)*

THIS WEEK

KATE WINSLET

Did spoons play a major role in your childhood?

No, we could never afford spoons. We only had one, which all of us kids had to share. We were allowed to lick it, as a special treat, on Christmas Day after Dad had dipped it into a cup of tea without milk or sugar – or tea.

I'm sorry, isn't that straight out of Monty Python's Four Yorkshiremen sketch?

Nay, lad. We were too poor to afford Monty Python sketches. We used to dream of watching Monty Python sketches. There were 27 of us in t'corner of room watching a cardboard box *pretending* it were Monty Python.

Could I just return to the subject of spoons? Do you have many spoons now?

Well, yes, I do, obviously. I've been jolly lucky to make enough money to buy, you know, a few spoons, and I'm not embarrassed about it, but it wasn't always like that. We weren't middle-class, you know. We were a working-class family and I was perfectly happy with an imaginary spoon. You see, we were proud, lad, even though we were poor.

I'm terribly sorry, Ms Winslet, but you seem to have gone back into the Monty Python sketch...

You try telling that to the young people of today and they won't believe you. They won't.

Has anything amusing ever happened to you in connection with spoons?

No. We were working-class. We couldn't afford a sense of humour. Thank you! Ciao! Gotta dash! Bless! Gather! Whoops!

Highlights From The Greatest Arts Show Of All Time

Picasso told the Cumbrian colossus: "Milord, we have so much in common, you and I – wine, women and money!"

Composer Brahms told Melvyn: "It was worth writing all those symphonies just to get on your show."

The Bard of Avon told the Bard of Wigton: "TV or not TV – that is the question, eh, Melve baby?"

SWINE FLU
Your Questions Answered

Q How do I know if I've got it?

A You will experience flu-like symptoms, such as a runny nose or a cough. You may even have a sore throat.

Q Is that all?

A In the early stages, yes. But as the disease takes hold, you may experience more severe symptoms, such as death.

Q What should I do if I catch it?

A If you think you have caught swine flu, it is most important that you should avoid any further contact with human beings. Do not leave your home, do not cough or sneeze and, above all, do not visit your doctor. He or she has a very important job to do in looking after the victims of swine flu and it is therefore vital that he or she remains healthy.

Q What exactly is swine flu?

A Swine flu, or HGVINIOU to give it its proper medical name, is a variation of the common flu virus DVD5H6 which, though currently treatable, could well cross with avian and human strains of flu to form a more virulent strain, PGT1PS, which could well wipe out the entire human race within a week.

Q Should I panic?

A At present there is no need to panic. But should the present very alarming situation continue, panic may well be the most appropriate response.

Q Can I still eat sausages?

A At present there appears to be no serious risk in consuming pork products, so long as certain basic hygiene precautions are followed – e.g. hands must be washed three times with an approved biological hand-cleaner containing polyurethanedioxyribonucleicflaminate B.The towel you use to dry your hands must then be burned. The sausage must have been kept in a sterile environment for a minimum of 6 days before cooking. Similar precautions should be taken with the following foodstuffs: BLT Sarnie, Melton Mowbray Pie, Ham Roll, Pork Scratchings, Peregrine Worsthorne.

Q Is it essential to wear a face mask at all times?

A Yes, except when eating a sausage (see above).

Q Does Tamiflu work?

A Yes and no. In some cases it does, in other cases it doesn't. But the government has stockpiled over 2,000 billion doses, more than enough to kill the whole world. *(Is this right? Ed.)*

Q What is the correct response to someone sneezing?

A You should immediately reply with the traditional German expression 'Schweinflu!' (Bless you!)

"I'm afraid you've got dirty rotten swine flu"

THE 2009 VERSION OF THE POSTER THAT EVERYONE WANTS!

KEEP INDOORS AND CARRY ON PANICKING

"Alright, have it your way... you heard a pig sneeze!"

WILL SWINE FLU CAUSE NEW HOUSE PRICE CRASH?

HEALTH experts last night warned that a dramatic house price crash might be imminent in Britain in the wake of the global Swine Flu pandemic, as whole cities had to be abandoned by the authorities in the vain hope of containing the plague as the bodies of the millions of dead were left to rot in the streets, causing property prices in already depressed parts of the country to sink to new record lows and *(cont. p. 94)*

School news

St Cakes
The school has been closed after the Head Girl, Tammy Flu (Virals) returned from a half-term holiday in Cancun, Mexico. All pupils have been sent home, except the overseas boarders who have been locked in the sanatorium under 24-hour guard by Matron, Mrs Pam Demic RCN. Sneezers will not be run on June 3rd over Swine Field. There will be no performance of 'Porky and Bess' by the Drama Society on June 12th. St Cough's day will be cancelled, including the prize-giving. Apologies to the Speaker, Rt. Hon. Douglas Hogg O.C. The Leavers' Party will now be a Masked Ball held in the Nightingale Wing of St Swinian's Hospital. The Bursar, Major O.T.T. Panic, regrets that there will be no refund of fees already paid in advance by parents. Exam candidates will not sit the papers, but will be awarded their predicted grades (A*s for all pupils, as predicted by the Headmaster yesterday).

Lives of the Saints and Martyrs No. 94
St Joanna of Lumley

ANDTHERE was living in those times a beautiful, high-born lady named Joanna of Lumley. With her radiant smile and angelic voice, she enchanted all who saw her. One day she came across a humble gurkha sitting by the roadside, cutting nettles with his kukri knife to make nettle soup. For he was so poor that this was his only form of sustenance.

The kindly Joanna knelt down beside him and said, "You poor little gurkha. How came you to this sorry pass?"

And the gallant little warrior replied in his own language, "After all I have done for Britain, they are sending me back to gurkhaland where I shall surely die, for there are no nettles there for me to make my soup."

Hearing this sorry tale, the saintly Joanna at once determined to lead a great pilgrimage to Westminster, there to upbraid the wicked rulers of the land for their heartless crime.

And when she appeared, the mere sight of her melted the hearts of all who gazed at her, except one, the evil first minister, Gordon Brown.

And the cruel ogre told the poor gurkha, "I give not a fig for your sufferings – you must go back to the land where no nettles grow."

And when the people heard this, they cried out aloud that Gordon was a ruthless tyrant who must resign at once, to be replaced as first minister by the beautiful Saint Joanna.

ABSOLUTELY FATUOUS

Whatever you say, Your Majesty

A message from the Mayor of London
Boris Johnson

Boris's Wizard Wheeze

What ho, Londoners! How about this for a first-rate boffo idea? Forget the Bendy Buses – we're going to fill London's streets with millions of those little electric car johnnies! Just think, no smelly petrol fumes, no growling engines, and everyone zipping about, happy as Larry at 5mph! That's brilliant, BoJo, I hear you say. So London's going to lead the world in saving the planet. Correct! Brownie points to Boris – or should I say 'Greenie points'. And certain other Tory leaders looking a bit silly! (No names, eh, Dave?) He may have got a First, but certain other chaps from Eton have turned out to be a lot brainier when it comes to inventing the electric car and saving the world!

And how does it work, I hear you ask? Simple. Just like your mobile– just plug it in and some gorgeous tottie rings you up – whoops, I mean your wife, tells you to pick up some carrots on the way home.
Anyway, where was I? These cars. Fantastic! They run on solar power with a wind turbine on top, and all for free. I may not have got that bit right. I leave all the technical stuff to the boffins.

Cheerio!

Boris

"BoJo – Working For A Switched-On London"

New Green Electric Car

THE DAILY TELEGRAPH

Letters to the Editor

Ayo Gorkhali!

SIR – As one who has served out East, I yield to no one in my admiration of Johnny Gurkha. No finer fighting man exists than this fearless little fellow from the mountains of Gurkhistan who, armed only with his legendary Kukri knife, strikes fear into the heart of any enemy on earth.

I well remember leading a company of these incomparable warriors into the jungles of Shawaddy-waddy, where we were set upon by a whole division of Kamikazi Japanese tanks. At the end of the day, the casualty figures told their own story. Jap tanks 4,302. Gurkhas, nil.

I therefore hesitate to take issue with such a distinguished champion of the little fellows as Mrs Joanna Lumbago, who won all our hearts by her performance in the New Avengers (which, if I may digress for a minute, were nothing like as good as the original Avengers, starring the incomparable Diana Rigg). but it is a grievous mistake, in my view, to think that Johnny Gurkha could be happily transplanted to the countryside of the Home Counties, which to him would be an alien and hostile environment compared with the sunlit snow-capped peaks of Mount Everest, where he can hunt for his beloved yeti meat and die happily of frostbite in the land where the sun never sets (or is it 'never comes out'? – I've never been absolutely sure on this point!).

To sum up,
Yours faithfully

Sir Herbert Gusset
(Maj-Gen. Retd)
C/o Saloon bar, The Slug and Gherkin, Dunkillin, Wilts.

Dave Snooty AND HIS PALS

WE DISCOVER AMAZING REVELATIONS ABOUT MPs' EXPENSES

by Nick Story

PAINSTAKING research by this newspaper has uncovered the extraordinary story that is on the front page of the Daily Telegraph every morning.

Our team of top investigative journalists uncovered the truth behind Parliament's traditional confidentiality by painstakingly sifting through hundreds of columns of details contained on pages 1-94 of the Daily Telegraph.

But did money change hands?

The editor of this paper is, of course, reluctant to reveal our sources, but he is not ashamed to admit that he bought the information from a trustworthy newsvendor (a Mr W.H.S.). "I did not pay the ludicrous sums that are being bandied about. In fact, the amount I paid is close to 90p *and* I got a free bottle of water, which is a pretty good deal when you consider the public interest involved."

What you will read tomorrow: *We don't know because the Telegraph hasn't come out yet.*

OPINION

THE spectacle of greedy men and women lining their pockets with the proceeds of falsified expenses and unwarranted allowances has sadly gone from Fleet Street for ever.

That is why it is so annoying to see all those MPs still at it. How dare they? That's our job. Or it was until the bloody bean-counters cut everything. I mean, it's got so bad I'm not even drunk when I'm writing this. What sort of journalism is that? Come on, Mr Managing Editor, let me at least take one of my colleagues out to lunch and put him down as "senior political contact"!! Bastards!

© All newspapers.

CALL FOR CONVICTION POLITICIANS

AS THE political world teetered on the brink of complete collapse, there were nationwide calls for "politicians with convictions".

Said a spokesman for the newly-formed Voters Alliance, "The sooner we get these convictions, the better – I'm thinking five years for fraud."

He continued, "The sooner we get our MPs locked up behind bars the safer we will all be."

But last night the chief of Britain's prisons lashed out at what he called "these lunatic proposals".

"Britain's prisons are full of honest, decent criminals. I do not want them mixing with low-life MPs who will be a harmful influence on them and will almost certainly set them on a lifetime of crime."

"What's that you've got, Flipper?"

TORY RESIGNS

Duck off!

SPEAKER SHOCK

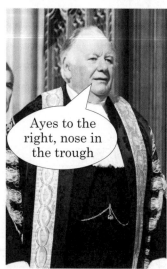

Ayes to the right, nose in the trough

"Can I have a receipt?"

Duck At Centre Of Political Storm

by Our Westminster Staff Huey, Dewey and Thirsty Will Lewie

A HAMPSHIRE duck was yesterday accused of claiming public money to fund his lavish second duck house whilst actually having a number of other undeclared residencies in ponds and lakes around the country.

Mr Duck angrily denied any impropriety, claiming he had broken no rules.

When pressed, he admitted that taxpayers' money had been used to clean the moat around the recently refurbished duck house, and that the residence had actually been used by his daughter Jemima. "But there is no question of fowl play," he said.

Following calls for Mr Duck to be shot and roasted, he told local reporters: "Everyone else is just jealous because my Duck House is very large and looks like Duckingham Palace."

Mr Duck yesterday – keeping a low profile

However, BBC Royal Reporter Rose Mallard said that the house looked nothing like (Cont. p. 94)

Lines Written On The Resignation Of Speaker Martin

By WILLIAM REES-MCGONAGALL *(Nominated By Sean Connery As Scottish Poet Of The Millennium)*

'Twas in the year sixteen hundred and ninety five
That Sir John Trevor, speaker of the House of Commons, was still alive.
But, alas, he was found guilty of a high crime and misdemeanour
And I'm not just talking about paying your brother for your cleaner.

Sir John was dragged screaming from the Speaker's chair
In front of all the MPs who were gathered there,
But the nation then had a very long time to wait
Before another Speaker was to suffer a similarly ignominious fate.
Three hundred and fourteen years to be exact
Before the next Speaker had to be humiliatingly sacked.

Michael Martin was this miscreant's name
Who brought his office into unparalleled shame.
He was known unkindly as 'Gorbals Mick'
Merely because he was working class Glaswegian and very thick
                        (surely 'Roman Catholic'? Ed.)
Mr Martin had presided over an avalanche of sleaze
Which had been freely indulged in by almost all the MPs.

It seemed they had taken leave of their senses
When it came to claiming outrageous expenses.
As each day unfolded, the revelations grew more obscene –
One of them even claimed for an £8,500 telly with a plasma screen.
Another defined the very heights of excess
By making taxpayers pay for a Corby De Luxe trouser press.

And that was just Labour, but the Tories had no cause to gloat
For one of them had claimed for the cleaning of his moat.
Mr Douglas Hogg was this man's unfortunate name
For getting snouts in the trough was the nature of the game.

Even the Lib Dems were not immune
With finger pointing at Mr Christopher Huhne.
And though you would expect his motives to be finer
Sir Ming Campbell had claimed for an interior designer.

And so it went on, this roll of shame –
It seemed scarcely any of them were free from blame.
And as these horrors came to light
Speaker Martin became ever more uptight.

For he had tirelessly worked for many years
To prevent such scandals reaching the public's ears.
And he himself was far from squeaky clean
For his wife's visit to Tesco he had claimed for a hired limousine.

And when the press began to rake the muck
He called, in at our expense, Messrs Carter-Fuck.
But the Speaker had misjudged the mood of the nation
Which was one of furious indignation.

The entire country was now united in anger
All the way from Lowestoft to Bangor.
Still this Caledonian clown clung onto his job
For it was worth to him more than a wee few bob.

Plus a luxury apartment – not to mention
An enormous gold-plated and index-linked pension.
"I will nae 'gang awa'," he told the MPs
As they put down motions saying "Will you resign, please?"

But finally there was a knock at the door and there stood a man with a frown,
This late-night caller was none other than the Rt. Honourable Gordon Brown.
"The game is up my fine Scottish friend.
For you, Gorbals Mick, this is the end."

And so it's the end too for this epic verse
For of all the speakers in English parliamentary history not one had been worse.
(With the possible exception of Sir John Trevor,
Though on second thoughts I think Martin was the worst ever.)

*"Nonsense, man! Of course you're entitled to put down **all** of Dorset"*

"Sales are slow today"

"Thinking of dissolving parliament, Your Majesty?"

*"You are not going out dressed like **that**, young lady!"*

Let's Parlez Franglais!
avec Kilometres Kington

Numero 94
Le soixante-cinquième anniversaire de D-Day

(Une plage in Normandy. Le sixth June)

Le Prince de Wales *(pour c'est lui)*: Bonjour, M. Sarkozy.

Président Sarko: Qui est vous, matey?

Le Prince: Er, er... je suis le prochain King d'England.

Sarko (examinant le clipboard): Non, vous n'êtes pas sur le guest list.

Prince: C'est vraiment appalling, dans un vrai sense. J'ai no need d'un invitation-thingy. C'etait *nous*, les Anglais, qui avons liberés la France.

Sarko: Non, non, non, Monsieur Rosbif! J'ai vu Saving Private Ryan. C'était les Americains sous le fameux general Tom Hanks qui ont defeatés nos amis les Allemands.

Prince: Je don't believe que je suis hearing this!

Sarko: C'est absolument vrai! Vous pouvez visiter Obama Beach où les Americains et notre General de Gaulle ont made histoire et liberated le whole d'Europe.

(Entrez le grand President Obama)

Obama: Why, good evening, y'all. What a lovely little country you have here in Europe. Who are you two guys?

Prince: Je pense qu c'est temps pour retourner à Highgrove pour parler aux fleurs.

(Exit le Prince)

Sarko: Ah, Monsieur le Président. Bienvenu à mon humble celebration de D-Jour. Mais où est votre femme, Michelle? Quelle craqueuse. Une vraie routy-touty, n'est-ce pas? Même plus sexier que ma petite Carla!

(Entrez Carla)

Carla: Je heard that! Vous êtes en grand doo-doo.

Obama: It has been nice visiting with you folks. I think it is time for me to return to the White House. Have a nice D-Day!

MAN GIVEN NEW FACE
Amazing Medical Breakthrough

Lines Written On The Appointment of Mr Scott Rennie As The First Openly Gay Minister In The History Of The Church Of Scotland

By William Rees-McGonagall

'Twas in the year of our Lord, two thousand and nine
That the Kirk of Scotland changed its former hard line.
For centuries under the dictates of the stern John Knox
They had told their ministers very firmly what they
could and couldn't do with their *(cont. verse 94)*

© W. Rees-McGonagall

"I hate it when Dad dances at parties – it's so embarrassing"

●Exclusive to the Daily Telegraph and all other newspapers.

MP Denies 'Flip-Flop' Claim

INVESTIGATION
THE EXPENSES FILES DAY 994

by Telegraph Expenses Team
C.D. HACKS

LIB DEM backbencher Barry Beard, MP for the Cornish constituency of Polzero, last night reacted angrily to the Daily Telegraph's sensational revelation that he had attempted to claim a £2.99 pair of flip-flops on his House of Commons "Second Holiday Home" allowance.

The Fees Office, however, rejected the claim on the grounds that the "beach footwear" acquired from Old Jethro's Surf 'n' Dive shore-side emporium was not directly related to Beard's performance of his duties as an MP.

"I utterly repudiate these baseless allegations," said an outraged Beard last night, "and I will be stepping down at the next election."

Other incredible revelations about MPs' expenses on pages 2-94 in today's *Daily Telegraph*

● Luxury mushroom soup tin found in ex-Minister's wheelie-bin.

● MP's wife "bought new hat" – he said it was "within the new rules".

● Labour backbencher did not declare 10p piece he found on pavement.

Royal Family 'Can Talk To One Another' Claims Scientist

by Our Science Staff **Lynda LaPlante**

MEMBERS of the Royal Family are now thought to be able to communicate with each other, according to a new report published in the scientific journal 'Plants & Plantsmen'.

The article claims that new film shows members of the Royal Family swaying in the wind and appearing to nod at one another, indicating a primitive level of communication.

Says Professor Flowerdew of the Institute of Nutters, "We have a slow-motion recording of one of these organisms appearing to say 'What do you do?' or possibly 'Have you come far?'"

If shoplifters had the same rights as MPs

"You should resign, I've been doing this for years and you haven't stopped me before now"

CITY ATTACKS 'COMMONS BONUS CULTURE'

FORMER RBS boss Sir Fred Goodwin last night led attacks by senior disgraced City bosses over the culture of greed in the Commons.

"A culture of unparalleled greed appears to have become systemic within the House of Commons," Sir Fred told reporters from his yacht in Majorca.

"Greedy MPs need to understand the very real anger of City bankers who didn't get a slice of that."

POETRY CORNER

Lines On The Resignation Of Ruth Padel As Oxford Professor Of Poetry

So. Then farewell
Ruth Padel.

Unlike mine,
Your poems don't rhyme.

E.J. Thribb
Professor of Poetry at the
University of Twitter (formerly
Hay-on-Fry Polytechnic)

OXFORD POETRY CONTEST

We're up Shit Creek without a Padel

THE DAILY TELEGRAPH

Letters to the Editor
Painted Ladies

SIR – I have been following with great interest the many letters from your readers who have been astonished in recent weeks to see their gardens filled with painted ladies.

Alas, my own garden has not been graced by these exotic creatures, who, I am told, have come all the way from Africa to disport themselves on our lawns and sample our legendary British cream teas.

Nevertheless, as one who has been out East and seen a thing or two in my time, I have vivid memories of the painted ladies who in happier times were to be found in large numbers adorning the back streets of Kuala Lumpur.

I well remember one particular occasion when my adjutant Captain Frobisher and I were attempting to reach our club, Whites Only, for a spot of dinner and a quiet game of cribbage when we were waylaid by a dense flock of these painted ladies, insistent on providing us with the pleasures of the town. So pressing were they in their entreaties that we eventually succumbed to their invitation and, albeit reluctantly, joined them in the Kama Sutra Hotel at the junction of Lord Palmerston Road and Duke of Cambridge Avenue.

What happy days they were, and my only hope is that I can relive them this summer as these beautiful and delicate wonders of nature make a long overdue visit to the environs of Market Barkworth.

Yours faithfully,
Sir Herbert Gusset
Via email.

"And did those feet in ancient time..."

THAT BBC EURO ELECTION NIGHT SPECIAL IN FULL

Dimblebore *(for it is still him)*: And this really is the most extraordinary night of drama, even though most of the results are yet to come in. Emily, what's going on in Benelux?

Emily Maitliss *(for it is she)*: Well, David, I should stress that this is a Euro Election and not a General Election, so we can't extrapolate directly, but so far in Benelux the one result we have shows a swing away from the centre left parties like the Christian Social Democrats and the Democratic Christian Socialists.

Dimblebore *(nodding as if he is not asleep)*: And what about the centre right parties, Emily, such as the National Christian Democrats?

Maitliss *(points to large chart)*: Well, the projections are that their vote will fall because of widespread defections to the fringe parties, such as the ultra-rightwing Christian National Democratic Fascists and their rivals, the National Fascist Christian Democrats...

Dimbebore: I'll have to stop you there, Emily, because there is sensational news in from West Avon, that's a North-East country seat in Sussex, and it's an incredible victory for the United Kristian Independence party.

And if that were repeated at a General Election then UKIP would be forming the next British government. An incredible thought. Polly Toynbee, you've managed to stay awake... what's your view on this amazing result?

Polly Toynbee: Well, David, you have to remember that the turnout in West Avon was only 7% and UKIP only managed to attract 17 votes, but the fact that the Labour candidate was 7th in the poll behind the Eco-No-To-Plastic-Bag Party and the Pro-Viagra-Compulsory-Latin-In-Schools Alliance must act as a wake-up call to the Labour Party and...

Dimblebore: Sorry, we'll have to stop you, Polly, as Jeremy Vine has got some extraordinary news...

Jeremy Vine: Yes, our latest figures show that no one is now watching this programme. This is an absolutely unprecedented situation.

Dimblebore: So, what does this mean actually, Jeremy?

Vine: Well, David, it means we can all go home and read about the elections tomorrow in the papers.

(Closedown)

The Daily Telegraph

Friday, June 25, 2010

Tory MP Claimed 99p For Roll of 10 Bin Liners And Only Used 8

 INVESTIGATION
THE EXPENSES FILES **DAY 9,994**

by Our Commons Investigation Staff C.D. Rom and Phil Front-page

KEN SWIVEL, 54, who has been Conservative MP for West Mildew since 2005, was yesterday sensationally revealed to have once claimed taxpayers' money to fund an extravagant purchase of bin liners from the Market Barkworth branch of B&Q on 12 July 2007.

The story came to light as a team of 30 *Telegraph* journalists were engaged in what editor Will Lewis called "Operation Barrel-Scrape".

● Full story and exclusive pics of the B&Q liners that *you* paid for and *he* never used **6-8**

● "I am innocent," says Swivel, "and I shall be standing down at the next election" **10**

Exclusive To All Newspapers

Newspapers Give BNP Too Much Publicity

THEY ARE an insignificant and irrelevant party, representing a minute section of the electorate. They have just scored a minor victory in the Euro Elections. And yet, still newspapers devote huge headlines and acres of column inches to the British National Party in an attempt to scare their readers and persuade them that this pathetic group of extremists are much more dangerous than they actually are. With big pictures of Nick Griffin *(see above)* and huge Nazi swastikas to spice things up a bit these irresponsible newspapers are *(cont. pp. 2, 3, 4, 5, 6-94)*

"The expenses row has really put me off politics... so I'm going to vote for racism, bigotry and hatred instead"

A Pathetic MP   Apathetic Voter

"I got this little Polish chap I know to knock it up for me"

DIARY

PETER HITCHENS: THE INDEX

Aardvark: deliberately offensive animal genetically engineered by leftist medics 12-14

Andrews Sisters: high point of Western Culture, The 192-193

Ankles, Women's: high time they were covered up, or we all face a government-sponsored plague of venereal disease 27, 56

Angkor Wat: British monument pilfered by foreigners 78

Apples: Stalinist doctors determined to force-feed us an apple a day against our will 70-73

Arsenic, more poisonous than: *See* Blair, Cherie

Babies: gullibility of 54
inability to stand on own two feet 59
politically illiterate 55
whiners and whingers 56-7

Bananas: bent 93
bruised 94
yellow 95

Biscuit: unsavoury 12
'u' in word "biscuit" kept silent by our political classes 13

Blair, Anthony: and probable involvement in "unsolved" Jack the Ripper murders 203-7

Blair, Cherie: denies being fully paid-up Colonel in the KGB 202

Bosoms: far too many 121
Trotskyite plot to expose Jordan's 122
wholly gratuitous to mention them in this context 123-9

Brains, Fried with cannabis: *See* Young People Today

Broth: too many cooks improve the 51-2

Cameron, David MP:
banana, spotted secretly eating a 106
Blair, Anthony: possible homosexual liaison with 123
elitist pronunciation of "biscuit" 13
praise for mass-murderer Mandela 17
repeated refusal to admit involvement in burning of Reichstag building 190-92
tell-tale Leninist hair-do 14

Cheese: Exactly the same as chalk, despite what they may have us believe 91

Communist spies, probable: *See* Dench, Dame Judi; Edinburgh, Duke of; Potter, Harry; Tebbit, Norman;

Daleks: and New Labour 35-8
role in determining EC policy 38-41
secret 35-year alliance with Dr Who
See Who, Dr

Darling, Alistair MP: beard suggests possible transsexual 183-34

Eggs: Omelettes best made without breaking 29

Elm Disease, Dutch: Brought into this country in early Seventies by "pop" group The Rolling Stones with full knowledge of Buckingham Palace 177

Facts: simply not true 77-84

Farrakhan, Louis: welcomed as Treasurer of Henley Conservative Party 93

Fishfingers: contain cannabis 14, 46

Forsyth, Bruce: self-proclaimed homosexuals permitted on Strictly Come Dancing 134-7

G-Spot: government invention 67
ruse to distract us from Iraq war 68

Gander, Goosey-Goosey: homeless vagrant and sexual pervert 103

Gymnasium: paedophiles trained in government-funded: 119, 157

Hands: urgent need for gloves on women's 41

Homosexuality: soon to be practised between men and women 145-47

KGB: Tommy Cooper full Colonel in 199

Kindergartens *(origin: German)*: hotbeds of thought-control 98

Laxatives: forced on author by person or persons unknown shortly before major speech 222

Pan, Everything going down the: 1-229, 231-258.

Persons Unknown: David Cameron, Alastair Campbell and Cherie Blair 222

Quill Pens: banned for sale by extremist left-wing sectarians in WHSmith 112

Rugby Football: hot-bed of homo-sexuality 43-4

Run Rabbit, Run Rabbit, Run, Run, Run: or you will be preyed upon by left-wing Islamic pederasts 25, 34, 57-8, 92, 97, 109, 167-8

Scum of the Earth: *See* Wimbledon, Wombles of, The 223

Sexual intercourse: permitted by successive leftist governments 116
endorsed by Cherie Blair 117
seen on TV, Disgrace that it is 118-25
throughout the day and night, if you look hard enough 125-33

Sweet, Life is: no it jolly well isn't, at least not in my house 98-101

Tortoises: even they are having it away with one another, with no one bothering to stop them 133-4

Turtles too: 135

Up Up and Away In My Beautiful Balloon: *See* subversive long-haired songs that promote drug abuse 171

Vaizey, Ed: former member of The Village People 29

VD: kissing leads to 139

Winter: season before Autumn and after Spring 221-5

Young People Today:
brains addled through excess of depraved sex 112
elders, No respect for their 113
high on drugs 114
incapable of rational thought 115

XXX: *See* VD

Yo-Yo: blunt instrument employed by under-10s to terrorise police 212

Zigzag: only responsible way to drive along motorway at speed, but now forcibly outlawed by politically-correct police 219-20

As told to CRAIG BROWN

WIMBLEDON: SIX TO WATCH AND LISTEN TO

Grunta Snortavic
Russian 22-year-old with a wide range of off-putting noises. Probably one of the loudest players on the circuit.

Mona Grøna
Swedish 19-year-old with a deep bellow that opponents find very difficult to deal with.

Huffi Gruff
German 25-year-old whose rasping sighs have made her a favourite with no one at all.

Whoopee Screech
American 20-year-old, one of the all time greats, with a serve-and-volume game that makes her unbeatable at this level (94 decibels).

Penny Quiet
Soft spoken English 21-year-old – don't expect to hear very much of her *(That's enough)*.

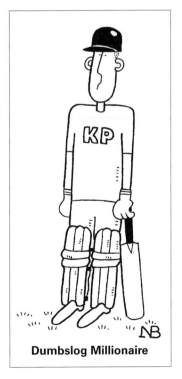

Dumbslog Millionaire

■ **CAROLINE FLINT!?!!** What a disgrace!?! So you think you look like Sophia Loren, walking out of the Cabinet on your high heels, a-poutin' and a-spoutin' about how badly Gordon's treated you!?! Not badly enough, darling!?! You've let us gals down with your whingin' and cringin' about so-called sexism!!? Cut out the bitchin' and snitchin', sweetheart, and if you think you look that good take a job on the catwalk – 'cos you're *catty* enough!?!? Geddit!!?

■ **THREE CHEERS** for Caroline Flint!?! She's the saucy sexpot who's waltzed out of Brown's dreary Boys-Own Bunker and given us gals something to cheer about!?! With your high heels and red dress, you look just like Sophia Loren!?!! Only better!!?! And it took a woman to tell gloomy Gordon where to get off!? You've done us all a favour, Caroline, with your salvo against sexism!?!! Tell you what! You should take a job on the catwalk – 'cos you're easily beautiful enough!?!!

■ **HAZEL BLEARS,** Jacqui Smith etc. What a disgrace!?! *(See above)*

■ **HAZEL BLEARS,** Jacqui Smith etc. What a disgrace!?! *(See above) (You're fired – Ed.)*

■ **HERE THEY ARE** – Glenda's Meltdown Munchies!?!

● **Nigel Farage.** UKIP's Number One Sex-Bomb!?! Tell you what, Nige, UKIP round my place from now on!?! Geddit?!!

● **Nick Griffin.** BNP's hunky Führer!!?! OK, so he's a fat fascist but a girl can't be too choosy these days!?!

● **Lord Falconer.** Former Lord Chancellor and Tony Blair's old flatmate, stoopid!?! Care to share a flat with a woman for a change, Big Boy!?!!

Byeee!!

"Thingummy's certainly made a name for himself"

LATEST RESIGNATION

Court Circular
Society Wedding

The Dot Cotton Suite, The Ramada Hotel, Staines

The Rt Hon Gordon Brown and the Rt Hon David Cameron yesterday attended the nuptials of Her Royal Highness The Grand Editrix of Wapping, Ms Rebekah Filth, to Mr Charlie Bookie of no fixed odds. The bride was given away by her employer The Digger of Dirt, who was accompanied by his consort, Wendy Oldmansnuffsitgetthelot.

The bridesmaids, Kelly Whoppers, Shelley Knockers and Melly Boobs, wore thongs kindly supplied by the Ann Summers World of Sex Emporium.

The Worst Man was Sir Piers of Moron, representing the Burger King Scent Co, and the couple were driven away by Mr Jeremy Clarkson in the new Bugatti Viglen at 197 mph into the nearest tree *(shurely shome mistake)*.

COULD WHEELIE BIN NIGHTMARE CAUSE HOUSE PRICE MELTDOWN?

by Our Rubbish Staff

Britain was last night staring into the abyss as a menace far worse than swine flu, global warming, economic collapse or the end of democracy as we know it threatened every homeowner in the country.

The mass revolt sparked off by the Daily Mail's great wheelie bin campaign brought thousands of people onto the streets calling for an end to the tyranny of the 'wheelie bin czars'.

Waving placards calling for an end to fortnightly collections and different coloured bins to separate waste streams, the real worry of the demonstrators was expressed by a typical 61-year old house-owner, Paul Dacre, who last night told the Mail, "You can't sell a house with row of bins blocking the drive. It wipes £60,000 off the price overnight. I am staring negative equity in the face, thanks to the little ayatollahs in my town hall."

Full story and pics pp. 2-93.

MAIL COMMENT

They are unsightly and full of terrible garbage, so why are more and more copies of the Daily Mail being left in the street when they should be thrown away in a wheelie bin where *(cont. p. 94)*

SUN OFFICIAL WEDDING PHOTOGRAPH

Come on, darlin' – get 'em out for the lads!

That Wedding Breakfast In Full

Freud Eggs
(Sun Side Up)

Red Top Slapper

Currant Bun (Stale)

To drink:

Choice of champagne
(Tittinger/Bums)

That Service In Full

Vicar: You may now kiss Mr Murdoch's bottom.

All: Yes, please!!

Prince Charles's Vision For Old Chelsea Barracks Site On King's Road

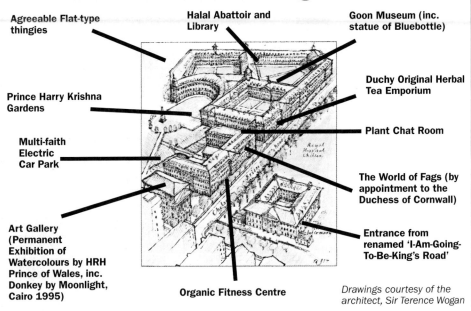

Agreeable Flat-type thingies

Halal Abattoir and Library

Goon Museum (inc. statue of Bluebottle)

Prince Harry Krishna Gardens

Duchy Original Herbal Tea Emporium

Multi-faith Electric Car Park

Plant Chat Room

The World of Fags (by appointment to the Duchess of Cornwall)

Art Gallery (Permanent Exhibition of Watercolours by HRH Prince of Wales, inc. Donkey by Moonlight, Cairo 1995)

Entrance from renamed 'I-Am-Going-To-Be-King's Road'

Organic Fitness Centre

Drawings courtesy of the architect, Sir Terence Wogan

WILLIAM SHOWS ROYAL CONCERN

You need to calm down about the architecture, Dad... There's steam coming out of your head

---

The Guardian Friday June 26 2008

Letters and emails

Chelsea Barracks

Dear Sir,
Am I alone in being sickened and outraged by the totally unwarranted intervention of Prince Charles in a private planning issue which is in no way his concern? Using his status as so-called heir to the throne, not to mention being obscenely rich, this arrogant member of the privileged elite thinks he has the right to impose his personal taste on the public in a way which is a flagrant affront to everything which democracy stands for.

The ultimate tragedy is that, thanks to the Prince's shameless manipulation of the Royal old boy network, London now stands to lose an architectural masterpiece by the world's greatest living architect, Richard Rogers, who has given us some of the most iconic buildings of the past half century, such as Lloyd's Building, the Pompidou Centre and... er... not only will thousands of people be made unemployed but the lack of affordable housing in Chelsea could create social problems well into the next century and beyond, all due to the over-inflated ego of a single self-important and un-elected megalomaniac.

Yours sincerely,

Les Corbusier
Corbusier Associates
The Old Bauhaus, Chiswick

THE DAILY TELEGRAPH Friday, June 26, 2008

Letters to the Editor

Chelsea Barracks

SIR – Am I alone in being sickened and appalled by the arrogant and high-minded conduct of Lord Rogers over a public planning issue in which he is professionally involved?

Using his status as a peer of the realm, a top government advisor and darling of the media, this arrogant member of the privileged elite thinks that he can impose his own personal taste on the public in a way which is a flagrant affront to everything which democracy stands for.

The ultimate victory for common sense, thanks to the courage of the Prince of Wales in persuading his fellow Royals to see the light, means that London will gain a delightful and very agreeable masterpiece by Sir Quinlan Terry Wogan, one of the greatest architects of this or any other age. The only person, it seems, who cannot recognise this is that over-inflated and un-elected megalomaniac Lord Rogers.

Inigo Gussett-Jones
Gavin St. Amp, Wilts.

THE MARAUDING MINISTERS MAKING A MELTDOWN!   Fountain and Jamieson

---

75

What You Will Read (In 2029)
That New Iraq War Inquiry

Parkway

Martin

Placeman

Lie

Rubbesh

Who are they – the four wise men (and one woman) who will finally tell us everything we know already about the Iraq war?

Lord Didcot of Parkway

Formerly Sir Charles Didcot, permanent secretary at the Ministry of Ministries. Lord Didcot has already served on several other inquiries into the Iraq War, concluding in each case that in a very real sense no one was to blame.

Sir Gilbert Martin

Immensely respected independent historian, author of the definitive 18-volume biography of the former Labour Home Secretary James Chuter-Ede. He once described President Bush and Tony Blair as "the Roosevelt and Churchill of our times, except better".

Sir Lawrence Placeman

Immensely respected independent historian, author of the official 24-volume study of The Foreign Policy of President Lyndon B. Johnson, once claimed to have put the idea of invading Iraq into Tony Blair's head, when he wrote a memorandum to Number 10 suggesting that Saddam Hussein should be "strung up – it is the only language he understands".

Sir Roderick Lie

Immensely diplomatic former Ambassador to Iraq, Sir Roderick has always been a tremendous admirer of Tony Blair, and has a long and distinguished record of "doing what I'm told and not rocking the boat, old boy".

Baroness Uttar Rubbesh

Immensely undistinguished, she has chaired hundreds of government bodies, including the Common-wealth Traffic Lights Authority, the Runny-Egg Marketing Board and the Joint Council of the Equal Opportunities Conciliation Service. She has been appointed because she can bring to the inquiry the unique qualities of being a) Asian and b) a woman.

The Report In Full

❶ Your committee was invited to investigate all aspects of the invasion of Iraq in 2003 and the subsequent occupation, to assess carefully all the relevant evidence and information relating to the above matters, to question those involved (when necessary in private), and to conclude that, while certain mistakes and miscalculations may have been made, no one was to blame in any way.

❷ Er...

❸ That's it.

In the interests of national security, the findings and contents of this report will not be released to the public until after the General Election or 2500 (if sooner).

Signed

DIDCOT OF PARKWAY
SIR GILBERT MARMITE
SIR LAWRENCE OF ARABIA
SIR RODERICK SPODE
THE BARONESS UTTAR RUBBESH
GORDON BROWN

Satellite TV Highlights

Father Ped *Dave, Friday 9.30*

Classic episode where the Bishop orders Father Ped O'Phile to set up Craggy Island's first children's home, with the usual hilarious mix of child abuse, strange priests and child abuse.

Eye Rating *You will apologise eventually, Father, you will, you will, you will, you will.*

BBC Radio 3

Opera Highlights

Muammar Mia! by Berlusconi

CLASSIC *Opera Buffooni*, which opens with the Robber Baron Silvio cavorting in the Palazzo Fornicazione with a chorus of scantily clad nymphs who sing the chorus *"Money, Money, Money – We've Come Here For The Money"*.

Suddenly, the sound of trumpets heralds the arrival of a mysterious visitor from Africa. It is the ruler of Libya disguised as a humble colonel. He reveals his identity in the aria *"Sono Looni Gaddafi"*.

Silvio is thrilled to receive a visit from such a mighty potentate and welcomes him, singing *"La Donna e Mobile"* (*"I can ring up for some more girls"*). Gaddafi is dismissive of this offer, and tells his new host that he has brought plenty of girls with him, in the form of his bodyguard made up of 1,003 virgins (*"Mille e tre"*).

Silvio laughingly responds *"Notta forlonga"* (*"They won't be for long"*).

The two men retire into the palazzo accompanied by twin choruses of *"Nymphs"* and *"Bodyguards"* to discuss the affairs of a neighbouring African state (*"Conversazione diplomatico di Uganda"*).

BRITISH MOVIE 'NOT TO BE SET ON COUNCIL ESTATE'

THERE WAS shock today in Cannes after it was confirmed that a new British film wouldn't be set on a depressingly grim council estate filled with single mums and violent, thuggish chavs.

"We've decided instead to set it in a depressingly grim Soho Private Members Club where everyone is trying to sell new British films set on depressingly grim council estates filled with single mums and violent thuggish chavs," said a man in a black t-shirt.

... I lay the blame for this epidemic of false names firmly at your door.
JACK HUGHES.

... Frankly, we would have thought at this time of year that people should be in church rather than writing time-wasting and silly letters.
FATHER CHRIS MASS, CAROL SERVICE AND MISS L. TOE.

... I am very grateful to your organ and the numerous attempts by your readers to cheer me up during the winter months. Unfortunately, it hasn't worked.
SARAH TONIN.

... As a reader from the UAE, I am confused as to why your readers would send in letters to you with obviously made-up names.
This would never happen in my country.
SHEIKH YOURBOOTY.

...... Over the last few months you have featured letters from correspondents signing off with false names for intended humorous effect. At first this was fairly amusing but the longer it continues, the less it works. Let this be the last word on the matter.
LAURA D. MINISHINGRETURNS.

... I believe this pseudo name silliness should be drawn to a close.
ANNETTE CURTAIN.

... No more anonymous letters please.
ANNE ONNYMOUS.

... This puerile correspondence featuring obviously false names is threatening to take over the magazine.
It is driving me mad – so much so that, were I a subscriber, I might threaten to cancel.
IT MUST STOP!!!
ARFUR FFOULKES-AYCKE..

● Due to the large number of complaints received, this correspondence is now closed.

... Thank heavens you are to stop printing letters from people with silly names.
ABBOT FFIRKIN-THYME.

... I was disappointed to read of the demise of pseudo names. Some people clearly have no sense of humour!
MISS N.U. ALLREDDY.

... Unlike most of your recent letter writers, I thought the Pseudo Names section was hilarious and demonstrated the humour of the British public at their finest. My only regret was that I did not manage to send in a letter myself before the correspondence was closed.
MR BOAT.

... It's a pity that you closed the made-up names correspondence when you did – sooner or later one of them was bound to have been quite funny. Who says so? I do.
LAURA VAVRIDGES.

... Sad to see the apparent demise of the splendidly imaginative made-up names. What can I say?
SHAMUS O'LOHVER.

... Great to see you haven't given in to the whingers and continue to delight us with Pseudo Names. We especially like the international mix of the correspondence.
ATTA BOYKI, PAM CUMMING.

... Despite calling time on pseudonymous correspondence, we predict that it will run and run all year.

In anticipation we would like to wish your readers a White Christmas 2009.
MAJOR DAYS-BEE, MARY ANN BRIGHT, ANN MAY HALL, YORK RHYS, MRS B. WHITE.

.... I have been dithering about whether to join your Pseudo Names correspondence for several weeks. Am I now too late?
DILLIE TANTAY.

... Whichever edition finally brings an end to these ridiculous names, Oh Lord, I want to be in that number.
WENDY SAINSCO-MARCHENIN.

... As a very regular reader of your magazine for more years than I care to remember, I have a splendid idea for you – get people to write in with made-up names. Now, bet you never thought of that one!
AL ZHEIMER.

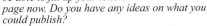

... Thank you for putting an end to the Pseudo Names correspondence. We've always admired your ability to stop repeating a joke before it gets dull. But we're worried that you might not be able to fill up your letters page now. Do you have any ideas on what you could publish?
ANNE DREW, NEIL INAVEST.

... We would like to thank the Editor for continuing the Pseudo Names column as we enjoy it so much!
FRASER JOLLY-GOODFELLOW ANN-SUSIE OLIVERS.

... When will it end? Your last issue includes a Christmas carol of made-up names – talk about dumbing down! What next? Nursery Rhymes?
C. SOAR, MARJORY DAWE, JOHN ESHALL, AVA NEWMASTER.

... I'd like to point out that the ancient Greeks had no such thing as a blender.
HOMER PLIANCE.

... Regarding Dillie Tantay's reasons for putting off writing to you about the Pseudo Names correspondence, I suspect her real reason was her amateur interest in the arts. The letter should actually have been signed by myself, her cousin.,
DILLIE TORY.

... Since mention of it closing (so glad it hasn't), I open each new copy of the Eye wondering if I am going to find my favourite bit, Pseudo Names, or not! Actually I quite like the element of suspense you have introduced.
CLIFF HANGER.

● That's enough Pseudo Names. Possibly. Ed.

... Eventually your Pseudo Names section will end. It will be sad, but what can you do...?
KAY SAYRAH.

... Please please don't axe this wonderful column.
FANNY S. SPART (no relation)

... I laughed so much at this week's silly names that I just had to sit down and have a nice cuppa.
T. STRAINER.

... I consider your Pseudo Name feature to be anti-Islamic – and I know where your correspondents live...
G. HADD.

● Er... Now I come to think of it, Mr Hadd has made a very good point. Perhaps it is time to end this correspondence. Ed.

... You should not be browbeaten into ending your Pseudo Names feature by threats from your correspondent G. Hadd. People like that should be locked up.
JUAN TANAMO.

... Re the Editor's suggestion in response to Mr G. Hadd's letter to end this correspondence. Should this occur, then it may well lead to further troubles.
CHRISTIAN UPRISING.

... The economy of the civilised world is wrecked and you expect us to make up silly names!
D. KLEINOFF, D. WEST.

... I do hope that this nonsense fizzles out before the summer.
BARBIE KEW.

... Please do not cancel Pseudo Names, it is my reason for living.
RAY ZONDETTE.

... So you have tried to bring the Pseudo Names correspondence to a close. We, the undersigned, think there may be trouble ahead.
BERT WEILL, DES MUHNLEIT, ANNE MÜSICH, ANN LOVE, ANDREW MANSE, LES FACE, DEE MÜSICH, ANNE DANCE.

... I agree with Mr Juan Tanamo (Pseudo Names, Eye 1234) that G. Hadd deserves locking up, but not in some namby-pamby holiday camp jail. I suggest he samples some of the techniques recently outlawed by Softy Obama.
WALTER BOARDING.

... With its silly names column Private Eye really is sinking to new depths.
LUCY TANIA.

... The continued publication of these letters simply encourages infantile behaviour and is bad for morale.
MAJOR LOOK, MAJOR STARE MAJOR LUCY, R. UNDERWEAR.

... Calling for an end to Pseudo Names is futile. We've had a discussion and feel the point of no return has been reached.
RUBY CONN and MADGE ENO.

... I'm sorry but I won't be able to send you any Pseudo Names for the next issue – I'm washing my hair.
TIM O'TAY.

... The constant dribbling of these letters in your magazine should be stopped.
CATH ETER.

... I enjoy reading your Pseudo Names section when not making phone calls on my journeys to and from work.
EAMONN D. TRAYNE.

... I strongly agree with Lucy Tania, and would like to renew my subscription forthwith.
MANDY LYFFE-BOTES.

... A friend of mine has just told me that the names appearing at the end of the letters in the Pseudo Names column are not real and are just made up. Is that true, as I can't believe it?
NYE EVE.

... A way to finish this column once and for all is to create a fictitious page in the magazine where you claim further entries will be continued.
PAIGE NINETYFOUR.

PETER PAN DEAD

by **Snow Black**

NEVERLAND was in mourning last night as news broke that Peter Pan, the boy who never wanted to grow up, had died.

Peter was greatly loved by generations of children whom he had entertained with his adventures amongst the stars (including the first star on the right).

But amidst the outpouring of grief there were some reservations about Peter's darker side. Said longterm friend Wendy Darling, 75, "People do go on about Peter hanging around nurseries and taking people's children, but I think it's time to forget all that Lost Boy stuff and remember instead the pleasure he gave us by flying around, fighting Captain Hook and moonwalking the plank."

Reports from Neverland insiders claimed that Peter had not been well and had become "a shadow of his former self".

Said close confidante Tinkerbell, 87, "In recent months he had become obsessed with the idea that he was Michael Jackson".

On other pages

● Captain Hook to sue Abercrombie & Fitch over "Discrimination" **2**

● Big Bad Wolf huffs and puffs before contracting Swine Flu and dying **3**

● Protest grows over Toad's plans to build windfarm in the willows **94**

What you read in all newspapers

MY FRIEND MICHAEL

by P. Brandy Umberelli

MICHAEL AND I became friends nearly 40 years ago. He was just a troubled kid, with a lot of problems.

But you could see at once that he also had one helluva lot of talent.

Over the years, I came to realise that behind the troubled façade was a warm, sensitive, loving, kindly, generous, warm human being.

What can I say? I just wish I had met him. And now it's too late.

What you didn't read in all newspapers

MAD PAEDOPHILE DEAD

YESTERDAY a 50-year-old mentally ill paedophile died in America.

URI GELLER 'PREMONITION CLAIM'

I predicted Michael would die just hours after it happened

Michael Jackson changed the face of Michael Jackson for ever

Exclusive Eye Picture Probe

When Tragedy Hit Planet Earth, Where Were You?

JOCASTA BALON, 22, hair stylist from Neasden. "My mum texted me at the salon – Michael Jackson's dead. I couldn't believe it. I told all the customers. They couldn't believe it either. It was unbelievable."

ANWAT BHAJI, 52, Balti House proprietor, also from Neasden, "I was watching television at the back of the restaurant, with my brother-in-law it came on as a newsflash. Michael Jackson is dead. 'Who's he?' said my brother-in-law. I couldn't believe it. It was unbelievable."

MELANIE MELDEW, 47, mother of three, also from Neasden, "The first I knew about it was when my son asked to borrow some money. 'Have you heard, Mum,' he said, 'the king of pop is dead.' I immediately put on Thriller and listened to it all morning. It was unbelievable. I couldn't believe it."

TRISH NOBBINGTON, 19, student at the University of Neasden (formerly World of Carpets). "We were in our tent at Glasto and one of the blokes from the tent next door came over and said, 'Have you heard, Jacko has passed on?' None of us could believe it, but Amy checked on her iPhone and there it was. We couldn't believe it. We immediately put Thriller on our iPods as a tribute and danced in the mud. It was unbelievable."

REGINALD VOLETROUSER, 75, retired philatelist from Neasden-on-the-Hill. "You were kind enough to ask me where I was when this chap died. I'm terribly sorry, I don't know who he is or, for that matter, who I am. It's unbelievable, I know, I can't believe it either."

Now you can tell us where you were when the world changed forever.

Just text, email or twitter your moving personal account and we'll use it to fill up our special 94-page Michael Jackson supplement, free with every copy of tomorrow's Eye.

MICHAEL JACKSON AND ME

The Rt Hon Gordon Brown

To me, Michael Jackson was a legendary entertainer and perhaps above all, a keen supporter of policy of reinvestment in people to help cope with this unavoidable economic downturn coupled with a renewed awareness of the need to rebuild our society for the 21st century. The man gave us the Moondance, in which he appeared to move backwards but went nowhere. He is a continued inspiration to us all.

David Cameron

It was a truly terrible shock to learn of the death of Michael Jackson. We have lost a tremendous talent and a great friend to the Conservative Party. I know that, if he were still alive, Michael would have joined me in condemning this increasingly incompetent and lacklustre government. I hope now that all parties can come together and join in a General Election as a mark of respect to this hugely talented guy.

William Rees-Mogg

It is fair, in my opinion, to say that Michael Jackson – one of the Indiana Jacksons – will soon get over this latest setback to his career. He has never allowed himself to be the victim of trauma or neurosis. He is, by all accounts, a robust and healthy young man, with a pleasingly straightforward outlook on life. It seems clear to me that, despite his reported death, he has rarely been in better shape. All the signs suggest that he will bring renewed vigour and panache to the fifty-or-so concerts he has planned for the O2 arena. Some commentators have predicted the cancellation of some or all of these concerts. My own view is that his premature death, such as it is, will interfere very little, if at all, with his innovative and undeniably popular song-and-dance routines.

As told to
CRAIG BROWN

"So, I understand you work in the public sector"

"I never really thought about it, I just assumed he'd get a job and find a place to live. But now with the recession..."

WIMBLEDON CROWDS APPLAUD BRITISH ROOF

by Our Tennis Staff **Ivor Topon**

AT LAST this country has a first class roof that can compete with the very best roofs around the world.

Roof mania

Yes, it's really true, after all the years of waiting, British roof-lovers have finally got a roof to cheer for.

Said one delighted spectator, "Come on, Roof!"

And when the moment came, the Roof performed brilliantly and went all the way. It didn't falter. It didn't fail. It didn't give up in the early stages.

Anyone for roofing?

No, the Roof eased its way effortlessly across Centre Court to deliver what the crowds were

waiting for – a world-beating British Roof that we could all get behind and be proud of.

On other pages

- Roof wins BBC Sports Personality of the Year **p2**
- Roof to be given MBE **p3**
- The girl who tamed the Roof **p94**

(That's enough, Ed)

GLENDA SLAGG
Britain's Number One Seedy?!

■ **GREAT TRAIN** Robber Ronnie Biggs!?!! Let the poor old boy out of jail, for Gawd's sake!?!! What harm will he do to anyone a-dribblin' and a-droolin' in his wheelchair?!?? One thing's for sure, he won't be robbing any trains in *his* state!?! And anyway it was all a long time ago and he's served his debt to society!?! OK, so he escaped from jail!!? Who wouldn't?!? Good luck to him, I say, and let's give Runaway Ronnie the freedom he so richly deserves – and while we are at it let's name a train after him!!?! The Biggsy Express!?! Non-stop Euston to Brazil!!?! Geddit?! All aboard!!?!

■ **RONNIE BIGGS** – what a disgrace!!?! The sheer cheek of the man, expecting us to let him out after what he did!?! And don't tell me he's paid his debt to society – he escaped, for Gawd's sake!?! Let him out and the first thing he'll do is go and rob a train – and probably beat someone senseless while he's at it!?! 'Cos villains like that don't change their spots!?! No, I say let him rot in jail. And whoever suggested naming a train after him, they should be locked up as well!?!!

■ **SPARE** a thought for Arlene Phillips – the Come Dancing dame they cruelly dumped!??!? And for why?!! Just 'cos she's the wrong side of sixty!?!! Now I've heard it all!?! If Agein' Arlene was a fat old fella, the BBC wouldn't dare!??! But since she's a WOMAN, she's been booted out the door and some teenage totty has waltzed off with her job!!?! Here's Glenda's vote – Strictly Come Back, Arlene!!?!!

■ **WHY ALL THE FUSS??!?** Just 'cos some old bag has been given the heave-ho from her telly job on "Strictly", we're all meant to start a-weepin' and a-wailin'!?!! Let's face it – Arlene was never any good anyway, a-bitchin' and a-snitchin' like some sour old schoolmarm with swine flu!!?! Here's Glenda's vote – Tan-Go Away, Arlene!?!! And Strictly Don't Come Back!!?!

■ **SEEN BRUNO?!??** Don't bother!? Sacha Baron Cohen thinks he's the funniest geezer on the globe, a-poovin' and a-woovin' in his skin-tight lederhosen!?!! Well, I've got news for you, Sacha – you're about as funny as Michael Jackson's death!??!!

■ **SEEN BRUNO?!??** Don't miss it!!?! It's the craziest, campest comedy ever!!?! And Sacha Baron Cohen is *hilarious*, a-poovin' and a-woovin' in his skin-tight lederhosen!!?! I've got news for you, Sacha – you're even funnier than Michael Jackson's death!!?!

■ *HERE THEY ARE* – Glenda's Heatwave He-Men?!

● **Buzz Aldrin.** OK, so he wasn't first on the Moon, but I like a man who comes second!?! Geddit?!?

● **Andy Murray.** OK, so you didn't win Wimbledon!?! But I love a loser!?!! New balls, please!?! Mmmm!?!

● **Antony Gormley.** Can I come round and have a go on your plinth, Big Boy!?! Geddit?!?

Byeee!!

Finding Emo

79

Fruity Girls Wear Fewer Clothes In Heatwave

Shock Survey Rocks Nation

by Phil Front-Page

IN AN amazing exposé of female flesh, the Daily Telegraph has learnt that putting fruity girls on the front pages is a sure-fire way of selling newspapers to middle-aged men on trains.

Said one commuter, "I thought that nothing could be more interesting than the Lib Dem MP who claimed for an extra Post-It Note on his second box file, but I was wrong".

He continued, "Phwoar! I say! Those girls really are quite fruity, particularly in the sunshine."

MOON LANDING REMEMBERED

Typical Americans, they invade and then go home leaving the place in a mess

40TH ANNIVERSARY OF MOON LANDING CONSPIRACY THEORY

THERE WERE celebrations right across the web today, as people commemorated July 22nd 1969 – the 40th anniversary of the first moon landing conspiracy theory.

"It was Huck Willoughby who stood up in the middle of a bar in Texas and said the whole thing had been cooked up on a sound stage in Burbank," said an over-excited nerd.

"Huck was the first man to point out that flags on the moon shouldn't flap in the wind. And he posted his suspicions on the door of his shed, because internet chat rooms wouldn't get invented for another thirty years."

"Of course you don't have swine flu, you ridiculous hypochondriac, now fuck off"

NHS EXTREMELY DIRECT

RGT

Nursery Times

Friday, July 24, 2009

CHILD CARER BARRED FOR REFUSING PAEDO TEST

by Our Criminal Records Staff **P.L. Travesty**

AN experienced London-based child-minder has been denied the right to work with children because she refused to be vetted by the new Independent Safeguarding Authority.

Ms Mary Poppins, 43, had been offered a post as nanny to an unemployed investment banker, Mr Banks, who had been laid off during the credit crunch.

When told that she could not be allowed to look after Child J and Child M unless she agreed to be checked out as a possible paedo, she said, "This is completely ridiculous and insulting."

The Home Office, however, insisted that its new measures were "supercalifragilistic-expialidocious" and were designed to end the evil of child abuse throughout the nursery world.

When told this, Ms Poppins opened her umbrella and flew away.

Duke Of York Promises 'Huge Surge' In Uphill Battle

THE Grand Old Duke Of York has pledged "as many men as are needed" for Operation Uphill and Downhill, currently under way in Helmand.

"I am talking about a very large increase in boots on the ground," said the Duke. "Possibly as many as ten men."

ON OTHER PAGES ● World's oldest mum dies, leaving children orphaned in shoe **2** ● Old Mother Hubbard forced to sell cupboard to pay for care home **3** ● "Me And My Spoon" by The Dish **94**

Ex-Speaker Martin Chooses His Coat Of Arms

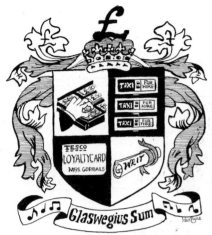

Glaswegius Sum

SHORTLY to be ennobled as Lord Gorbals of Sleaze, Mr Michael Martin has informed the College of Heralds to draw up his coat of arms as follows.

A shield quartered, bearing the following heraldic motifs:

1. A hand rampant gules in a till sable.

2. A trio of taxi meters bearing the legend 'For Hire'.

3. A Tesco loyalty card in the name of Mrs Gorbals.

4. A hand-inscribed libel writ drafted by Messrs Carter-Fuck, Solicitors and Commisioners of Oaths.

Beneath this shall appear Lord Gorbals's chosen motto, "Glaswegius Sum" enshrined on a musical stave.

News In Brief

ELECTION RECOUNT

THE Iranian Guardian Council has promised a full and fair recount in the number of protestors killed after the disputed Iranian election result.

"The widely derided initial figure of ten dead has been recounted, and the revised figure is now zero, since all the fatalities were responsible for their own deaths" said a heavily moustached man beating *(Cont. p. 94)*

Iran election results in full

Tehran North

Mahdman Ahmegeddon (Ruling Party)
3,937,403

Mir Hussein Moussavarecount (Losing Party) 2

No change ever if possible

HEADMASTER LASHES CHARITY COMMISSION

'Our only purpose is to serve community,' says Kipling

by Our Education Staff **Conrad Blackboard**

THE headmaster of the prestigious £64,000-a-term independent school St Cakes (motto: "Quis paget entrat") last night hit out at the Charity Commission for what he called "a politically motivated act of spite".

He was responding to the Commission's suggestion that St Cakes should lose its tax-exempt status after failing to provide sufficient benefits to the "wider community".

Said Mr Kipling, "This is ridiculous. St Cakes has a long and honourable record in serving any number of wider communities – the Russian oligarch community, the hedge fund community, the Chinese business community, and the African dictatorship community, to name but a few.

"Besides which, our school facilities have always been available to our local community. The squash courts, for example, can be hired out by anyone for a token charge of only £600 an hour during the hours between midnight at 5 a.m. (The key can be obtained from the Bursar, Major B. Ecclestone).

"So, to suggest that we should not enjoy 100 per cent tax relief is like saying that Mrs Kipling and I should not be entitled to our yearly three-month summer cruise around the Caribbean as a small token of all the work we put in to assist our participating stakeholders in the communities of which I speak."

News of Old Cakeians

M.V.Q. Onanugu *(Trousers 1971-1975)* has recently headed a military coup in Rumbabwe (formerly British Rumbabaland) and now holds the office of Supreme Life President and Commander-in-Chief. 'Monty' would like to make contact with any Old Cakeians who happen to be passing through Onanuguville (formerly Palmerston).

L.J.B. Smelt-Harris *(Smokers, 1968-1971)* tells us that he is serving a five-year sentence for fraud at the Barratt Open Prison in Fife, where he was delighted to run into fellow Old Cakeian, **R.B. St J. Halloran** *(Sliders, 1968-9).*

P.M. Brownlow *(Custards, 1991-1996)* wonders if he is the first Old Cakeian to marry another O.C. in a civil partnership. The "happy event" took place at the Chatsworth Court Hotel, Eastbourne, on January 7, 2009, when "Bunty" Brownlow and **C.J.R. Malfeasance** *(Pringles, 1996-2001)* "tied the knot".

P.M.D. Frossett (née **Mitchell-Webb**) *(Nightingale's 2000-2004)* has been appointed manageress of the Madame Provocateuse Adult Emporium in Bicester. Prunella is happy to offer a 10% discount to all Old Cakeians!

A Doctor Writes

Boar Flu

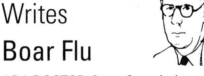

AS A DOCTOR, I am often asked, "Have I Got Swine Flu?"

The simple answer is No. You have Bore Flu or *Borus tediossissimus normalis*, to give it the full medical name.

What happens is the patient comes into contact with a newspaper report detailing the symptoms of Swine Flu. At once, the patient becomes a colossal bore telling everyone he's got Swine Flu when he hasn't.

This may cause intense drowsiness in all those listening to him and in some cases this could prove terminally dull.

If you think you have got Bore Flu, you are advised to stay at home and be quiet – ("Nil by Mouth")

© A. Doctor Norman.

"I think we need to get some new stock for this section"

THE DAILY MAIL SAYS

SAVE THIS POOR HACKER FROM PRISON

THE WHOLE nation is backing the Mail in its campaign to save a poor deluded hacker from being extradited from America and tried in the notorious British courts.

Rupert, 78, admits illegally hacking into the mobile phones of celebrities, politicians and Royals over a long period in his desperate search for a story he could put into his pathetic newspaper, the News of the World.

Doctors who have examined Rupert describe him as "just a sad fantasist, bordering on the autistic, imprisoned by his obsessions"

Rupert's devoted not-very-longtime partner Wendy Dung said last night, "It would be so unfair to put my Loopie in gaol, just because he publishes a lot of pornographic drivel in his newspapers."

"I need him here at home so that I can make sure that he takes a lot of exercise 24 hours a day and keeps his will up to date.'

Now you too can join the campaign to save Loopy Rupi by writing to the Home Secretary, whoever he or she may be at the time of writing.

HOW TO SAVE HACKER MURDOCH

▌Dear Mr Johnson (or it may
▌Lord Mandelson by the time
▌this reaches you, or possibly
▌Mr Balls or even Lord Adonis).
▌ I am very worried about
▌the possibility of Rupert
▌being unjustly extradited and
▌thrown into a stinking British
▌gaol until he dies, with
▌nothing to read but the Sun.

▌ Signed.......................

☐ I am over 18 and work for
▌News International

News in Brief

CELEBRITY OUTRAGE

HUNDREDS of high profile celebrities, including Stephen Fry and Jonathan Ross, said they were horrified last night to learn that News International had been intercepting their electronic communications.

"Every time we post some inane twaddle on Twitter, the very next day it's reprinted verbatim by lazy hacks in the showbiz pages of *The Sun* or the *News of the Screws*," said *(cont. p. 94)*

They're calling me a filthy old bugger

You're kidding!

SOLDIERS DIE IN WAR SHOCK

A NUMBER of British troops have been killed fighting in a war, the Ministry of Defence announced today.

Said a Ministry spokesman, "We deeply regret this shocking event. It is not the kind of thing you expect when you send soldiers off to fight."

ON OTHER PAGES
■ Should soldiers be sent off to fight in wars? You decide. Just text your verdict to 1357.

A Taxi Driver writes

EVERY week a well-known Cabbie is invited to comment on an issue of topical importance. This week **Bernie Ecclestone** (cab no. F1) on *The Virtues of Strong Leadership in Contemporary Politics*

ALL RIGHT in the back, guv? You can't see me cos I'm small, but I am 'ere, honest. Sorry I'm going so slow traffic's terrible tell you what that Hitler would have sorted it out don't get me wrong I'm not a Nazi or nothing but he did a lot of good he got the country going right who invented motorways? Hitler. So there you are – stands to reason Hitler was a very great man to my mind. If he was alive today I could get you to Heathrow in two minutes driving at 180 mph in the new Von Braun Formula One cab. Go! Go! Go! You know what I'd do with those people who get in my way, like that old lady in the Morris Minor in front? I'd string them up! That's what the Führer would have done. Not that I'm a Nazi but credit where it's due, guv.

I 'ad that Max Mosley in the back of the cab. Now there's a strong leader an' a very clever man. 'E would make a good prime minister, no seriously...

NEXT WEEK: Nick Griffin (cab no. BNP1) on the problems confronting Formula One Motor Racing in a Period of Austerity.

The Fidelio Telegraph

Friday, July 24, 2009

Deaf Musician 'Ends It All With Dignity'

by Our Man In Switzerland **Lunchtime O'Basel**

THE leading Viennese conductor and composer, Ludwig van Beethoven, travelled to Switzerland to "die with dignity" after years of worsening health.

Sir Ludwig, one of the biggest names in European music, has battled for a long time with deafness, hepatitis and an inability to finish his tenth symphony.

"His demons were many," said a close friend, "and Sir Lud made a brave decision to end it all, while he was still in full possession of his faculties (apart, that is, from his hearing, his sight and various other ailments).

"I know that if he had had

a wife, she would have been happy to pass on with him at the clinic."

The world of music was quick to pay tribute to the great maestro.

"Who is this Edward Downes?" they said. "We've never heard of him".

● Should Beethoven have been allowed to die with dignity? You decide.

If 'yes', text the word 'no' to 3456.

If 'no', text the word 'yes' to 5678.

CAMERON APOLOGISES FOR SECTION 28

> I'm a pretty straight kind of a gay

That Official Government Guide for Civil Servants Wanting to Use Twitter in Full

❶ Arrive at work.

❷ Sit at your desk and shuffle documents around to give off the impression you're actually doing some work.

❸ Log on to Twitter.

❹ Spend rest of morning reading what Jonathan Ross and Alan Carr had for breakfast, plus details of Stephen Fry's 'splendiferous bowel movements'.

❺ Receive 'tweet' from line manager warning you about inappropriate use of social networking sites during office hours.

❻ Turn off computer and do some work.

Thought For The Day
by
The Rev. A.N. Wislon

YOU KNOW, when I heard the news that the BBC's *Thought for the Day* slot might be opened up to non-believers, my first thought was, "I wonder whether the Daily Mail will ring me up and offer me a lot of money to write about it?" And, you know, in a very real sense, I was right.

© *Daily Mail Why Oh Why Productions*

● Was Andrew Wilson right to accept the money? Text 8253 for 'Yes', 9876 for 'No' and 6666 for 'I haven't got a thought in my head, but I'd like to share it with you anyway'.

CAMERON'S FOUR LETTER T-WORD GAFFE

by Our Absolute Radio Correspondent **DJ Taylor**

THE LEADER of the Conservative Party was left red-faced yesterday when he used an unacceptable four letter word during an interview for a popular music radio station.

David Cameron stunned aides by letting slip the word "Tory".

Cameron immediately realised his mistake but it was too late – the damage was done. Said one observer, "He was trying to be cool and with-it, but then he went too far

and blurted out a word that nobody wants to hear."

An embarrassed spokesman for Mr Cameron added, "David is very sorry if anyone was offended by the word 'Tory'. He did not realise that it has connotations that many people will find deeply offensive and is often used as a synonym for the C-word – Conservative.

"David did not mean to say that he was a Tory. He meant to say that he was a Twat."

Nursery Times

Friday, August 7, 2009

MR PUNCH CLEARED OF ASSAULT CHARGE

by Our Crime Staff **Scott Free**

TOP celebrity children's entertainer Mr Stevie Punch today walked from court as a free man after being accused of grievous bodily harm against Judy, the policeman, the crocodile and the little dog with the sausages.

The jury heard how Mr

Punch was "very famous and should be allowed to do whatever he liked". Giving evidence himself, Mr Punch told the court, "That's the way to do it!"

Gerrard's Cross

Yesterday his solicitor informed reporters, "Stevie will be celebrating with a big bash."

"He does the sign language for the deaf"

83

BROWN'S UNWINNABLE WAR

by Our Military Staff
MAJOR ERROR

EXPERTS are now agreed that there is no way that Gordon Brown can win his long-running war against the Toriban.

"He has spent billions," said one, "but to no avail. And in the process, he has lost an awful lot of not very good men and some really useless women (*Is this right, Ed?*)"

Under their new leader, the charismatic Bore Lord Osama bin Cameron, the resurgent Toriban have mounted a series of devastating attacks, capturing a lot of ground previously held by Brown.

"Morale is terrible," said one Labour veteran. "We don't have the personnel or the equipment to beat the Toriban."

Said another Labour foot soldier, "There is no clear statement of what we are trying to do here. Are we just holding on or are we part of a surge? No one seems to know."

The Camerons are Coming

But a defiant Gordon Brown was unrepentant yesterday. "We cannot just cut and run," he said, "just because we can't win. Besides, in recent weeks we have made some dramatic progress – backwards.

"This will make it much easier for us to regroup and launch Operation Massive Defeat next year."

ARMY EQUIPMENT SHOCK

Good news – there's no shortage of coffins

The Daily Chain Mail

— Friday 21 August 1346 —

100 YEARS WAR 'GOING WELL' SAYS GOVERNMENT

by Our Military Expert Professor **Normandy Stone**

THE conflict between England and France is "drawing to a close," said a spokesman for Edward III.

"It's been going for about 8 years now and although that may seem a long time to you, we've got to be committed to the long term, which might mean 100 years."

Asked about how the war would end, he said, "You can take it from me, it won't mean retreating back to England and losing all the territory we've gained".

● *Full story and unfunny tapestry by Robin Mahood* **94**

Who is winning in the battle for Afghanistan?

John Hutton

General Dannatt

Gordon Brown

Ministry of Defence

Man with Moustache
(probably Bob Ainsworth)

Gordon Brown's Tribute To Fallen Soldiers In Full

"THESE brave young men have made the ultimate sacrifice and, despite the fact that they never recorded a hit single or produced the fastest-selling album of all time or changed the face of popular music for ever, I still believe that their deaths are significant to millions of us.

Let us join together to mourn the sad loss of these soldiers who died without reaching their full potential.

They could very well have appeared having a racist strop on *Big Brother* or a blubbing meltdown on *Britain's Got Talent*, and could have had an individual and personal tribute from me, rather than this general one I'm doing now. *(That's enough. Ed.)*"

"Putting his telescope to his blind eye, Mr Brown said, 'I see plenty of helicopters'"

'Why Don't People Like Me? Is It My Moustache?' Asks Hitler

by Bob Ainsworth

DEFENCE supremo Adolf Hitler yesterday told the Eye that he was baffled by his widespread unpopularity.

"What is it about me that upsets people so much?" he asked.

"Is it my record running unpopular military operations during the war? Or is it my moustache?" *(cont. p. 94)*

 ON OTHER PAGES: Win a free **Bob Ainsworth** Novelty Moustache and amuse your friends and family! Ideal for Summer Barbecue Fun! Just answer the following question: *"Is Defence Secretary Bob Ainsworth even worse than Geoff Hoon?"* ☐ YES ☐ YES

The Daily Terrorgraph

Why we must fight on in Afghanistan

THERE has been a lot of criticism of our mission in Afghanistan. People ask what we are hoping to achieve, whether our tactics are correct and whether it is worth the loss of life to continue.

But if you ignore these arguments, one only has to look at the appalling way in which the enemy treats its own people to know that we in the Taliban must win at all costs.

This week we learn that they do not even respect the human rights of their own soldiers, refusing to compensate them for their injuries in the field and *(That's enough, Ed.)*

The Miliband Guide To Spotting A Moderate Taliban

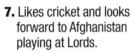

10 Telltale Signs

1. Only wears small beard.
2. Only carries small bomb.
3. Only met Osama bin Laden once.
4. Only prays four times a day instead of five.
5. Wives only have to follow three paces behind him not four.
6. Reads Guardian and votes Lib Dem.
7. Likes cricket and looks forward to Afghanistan playing at Lords.
8. Likes occasional G&T with his pork scratchings.
9. Admirer of Jeremy Clarkson's Top Gear.
10. Has never committed suicide.

(That's enough. Ed.)

NEW REPORT RECOMMENDS THAT ONLY EXPERIENCED BANKERS SHOULD SERVE AS NON-EXECUTIVE DIRECTORS

Great! I can start on Monday

Afghanistan
THE ROLL OF DISHONOUR 2001-2009

£40 BILLION HEIST IS BIGGEST IN HISTORY

by Our Crime Staff **Ronnie Biggestheistinhistory**

A GROUP of smartly-dressed men walked brazenly into the headquarters of most of Britain's leading banks and stole billions of pounds from under the noses of the financial regulators.

A spokesman for the police, Inspector "Knacker of the Fraud Squad" Knacker, said, "We are not investigating this blatant crime, though we have issued guidelines asking these well-dressed bankers not to steal so much money next time, as it didn't look too good for the industry."

Reuters, Aug. 2009.

"Bravo, young man! You remind me of myself when I was your age"

85

IN THE COURTS
Filth v. Whistle-Bower
Day 94

Mr Justice Eadycarrot *(for it is always he)*: Ladies and gentlemen of the jury, we have had an interesting few days, have we not, and you have heard a great deal of evidence concerning Mr Filth, one of our most respected newspaper proprietors.

Mr Filth is, in his own words, "a rough diamond", "a bit of a geezer" and "a very generous philanthropist donating large sums of money to various charities".

Other witnesses have attempted to introduce evidence to suggest a rather different story. They sought to link Mr Filth with the publication of what are often described as "adult" magazines and over-18 satellite channels, in the hope of lowering Mr Filth in your estimation.

That is why I have had to disallow any such evidence redounding to Mr Filth's discredit I quote the precedent of Maxwell v Truth, 1987. Notwithstanding the above, should I have inadvertently permitted any mention in this case of phrases such as "Asian Babes", "Big and Bouncy", "Teenage Nymphs at the Dentist", or whatever it may be, I must ask you to put it from your mind, however alluring such thoughts may be, particularly to male members of the jury.

No, ladies and gentlemen, you are only to consider the gravamen, the narrow question of whether or not Mr Filth intervened in the editorial direction of his newspapers. Again, you have heard clear evidence that he did. But you are equally to put this from your mind, whatever the learned imbeciles in the Appeal Court may, or may not have said, when they attempted to intervene in the direction of this court by pointing out that I had totally cocked it up.

As I say, I wish you to put all of this from your mind when you come to award Mr Filth huge damages in compensation for the impertinence of Mr Tom Whistle-Bower in

his grubby and salacious attempts to imply that Mr Filth is anything other than a saintly figure who is one of the greatest newspaper proprietors of this or, you may think, any other age. It is entirely a matter for you.

I would therefore ask you, ladies and gentlemen of the jury, to retire, as I myself will probably have to do, if those idiots in the Appeal Court get their way.

(The jury retired to find Mr Filth guilty as charged of being a seedy pornographer [Shurely shome mishtake? Ed.])

GOATS LEAVE SINKING SHIP

by Our Political Staff **Peter Obore**

THE captain of the Titanic, Gordon Brown, said yesterday that he was "very relaxed" about the abandoning of his ship by all the Goats whom he had brought on board to assist in the running of his liner into the iceberg.

In recent weeks the Goats (Government Of All the Twits) have jumped over the side rather than risk going down with Captain Brown.

Nanny State

Those Goats include:

● **Lord Digby-Useless**, former Head of the NBG.

● **Lord Malloch-Brownnose, former deputy head of the UNBG.**

● **Lord Darzehole, former high-flying Asian surgeon, brought in as expert on cuts.**

The only Goat still left on board is former admiral, Lord Westward of Ho, whose nautical experience has been invaluable in ensuring that the ship meets its navigational target, the iceberg.

Also still on board are a number of rats, chief among them Lord Mandelifeboats. *(That's enough rats and goats. Ed.)*

GOVERNMENT TO NATIONALISE BOTTOMLESS PIT

THE Government last night announced it was stepping in to nationalise a bottomless pit.

"We believe that this bottomless pit will prove to be a good longterm investment for the taxpayer, as we pour billions of extra pounds of public money directly into it.

"We hope to sell the bottomless pit at a later date back to the private sector at a knock-down price to maximise the losses incurred by the taxpayer."

LEMBIT SHOCK

We're having public relations

PALIN ATTACKS NHS

by Our US Staff **Lou P. Lew**

FORMER Republican vice-presidential candidate Sarah Palin has launched a stinging attack on Britain's NHS, saying that Hugh Laurie's medical genius was never recognised before his move to America.

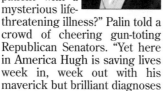

"All the time Hugh was working in England, did the NHS ever once ask him to diagnose a patient with a mysterious life-threatening illness?" Palin told a crowd of cheering gun-toting Republican Senators. "Yet here in America Hugh is saving lives week in, week out with his maverick but brilliant diagnoses on House.

"Only America's private health care could see what a brilliant surgeon Hugh Laurie was. God bless America!" said Palin, foaming at the mouth before being taken away by men in white coats.

"I'm afraid the idea of a free health service was too much for him"

AS IF the school "Hell-idays" weren't bad enough, now along comes Swine Flu to make the summer a total wash out – and I don't just mean two weeks of sodden "Staycation" in cloudbursting Cornwall with toddler Charlie complaining about getting rain in his pasty every day!!

No, when I woke up on Monday I felt sick and I had a massive headache – that's right, the au pair was ill! The selfish girl claimed she had Swine Flu, or Whine Flu, as I call it!

But I could tell our hopeless Chinese girl was faking it – she had none of the symptoms, except sneezing, a runny nose, a hacking cough, a slight temperature (104ºF), aching limbs, and diarrhoea and vomiting!?!

Aachu was obviously well enough to read up a few of the symptoms on the internet, but I wasn't fooled.

The government guide doesn't list inability to iron Simon's underpants or clean out the toddler's hamster cage as one of the main indicators of the virus, does it?

So before you could say Tamiflu, I had her out of bed taking Charlie to see Ice Age Three for the seventh time!!

Meanwhile, the Useless Simon also claims to have Swine Flu, lying around all day watching repeats of Stephen Fry's Extreme Weight Loss on UK Dave Minus Six (with special guest stars Dara Ó Briain and David Mitchell). But in the Useless Simon's case it's hard to tell if he's ill or not, since that's all he does all day anyway!! And how can Simon pick up a virus when he can't even pick up his socks from the bathroom floor? Like all other useless men! Aren't they useless?!! But let's forget them – it's not hard, is it?!! Where was I?

So, if you've got an outbreak of so-called Swine Flu in your au pair, here's Polly's guide to what you should do:

❶ **Quarantine**. Take yourself away from her immediately and book into a luxury spa for the weekend.

❷ **Face Mask**. They do a fabulous mud face mask at Pampers in Berkshire (only £795 per night, mud not included).

❸ **Wash Your Hands**. Yes, if she does persist in pretending to be ill, you should wash your hands of her completely and send her on the first plane back to her village in China! After Bird Flu they should be used to the odd pandemic!!

So, I think we've all learned one thing this week. Swine Flu is no joke. Though it is a column!!

© *P. Filler 2009.*

Opera Highlights

Berlusconi's I Prostituti-Frutti

Act One

THE curtain rises on the Robber Baron's lavishly furnished boudoir. Above the bed is a large gilt mirror. Photographs of the Robber Baron, accompanied by world leaders, decorate the walls.

Silvio is amorously engaged with the celebrated courtesan Rumpina Pumpina. She sings to him the moving aria *Mille e Tre* (*I'm yours for 1,003 euros, plus VAT*).

The Baron touchingly responds *It's a Deal*.

Rumpina urges Silvio to speak up and address his love-talk to her handbag, which she has strategically placed under the pillow.

Act One closes as Rumpina disrobes, while Silvio admires himself in the mirror and sings *Non Sono Santo* (*"I'm not a saint"*).

Act Two

IT IS the morning of the next day. A jubilant Rumpina, clutching her handbag, visits the offices of the newspaper *Il Nusi di Scruzi*. We see her handing a small tape recorder to the editor, while she sings the traditional Venetian folk song *Just one million euro, give it to me, delicious money from Italy*.

The editor, Signor Filthio, is only too happy to oblige and hands Rumpina a bag of gold ducats. He sings triumphantly *Bastardo Finito* (*We've got the bastard at last*).

Act Three

A SQUARE in Rome, the Piazza Margarita. The citizens are besieging the news kiosk for copies of *Il Nusi di Scruzi*.

From an upper window, the Baron looks down with trepidation, afraid that his reputation will soon be in tatters. He curses the treacherous Rumpina, singing *La slagga e Mobile* (*The crafty bitch recorded me on her mobile*).

But his anxiety turns to joy when he sees the male citizens saluting him with many a crude gesture, as they sing the rousing final chorus *Que Macho Stallione*, praising the 72-year-old Baron's virility and prowess.

Silvio descends to the street where he is carried shoulder high to a nearby bordello, where he is greeted as an old friend by a chorus of courtesans who sing *Cosi Fan Prostituti* (*We love you, Silvio, just like the men do!*).

Act Four

Silvio elected for a fourth term.

(That's enough opera. Ed.)

"You need to start at the bottom to get anywhere in this business, son"

The Alternative Rocky Horror Service Book

No. 94 The new "Three In One" Baptism, Marriage and Funeral Service.

The President *(for it is she)*: We are gathered together on this joyful but sad day to celebrate the life of this happy couple and to welcome into the church their children, to whom we offer our condolences on the sad loss of their parents. If anyone knows of any just cause or impediment why these persons should not be baptised, married and buried, they are to declare it now.

Hymn 94
"Three in one and one for the price of three."

The President: Who giveth this person to be buried?

The Children of the Deceased: We do.

The President: I now pronounce you baptised.

(The congregation may here applaud)

The Taking of the Photos

(At this point anyone with a camera, or mobile phone with camera facility, may step forward to take photos of the happy corpse)

The President: Do you renounce Satan and all his works?

The Deceased: I do.

(The organ shall now play a piece of suitable music – it may be the Wedding March [Mendelssohn], the Funeral March [Chopin], the Christening March [Lloyd Webber] or the Trumpet Voluntary Euthanasia [attrib. Jeremiah Clarke, arr. Downes])

The Sermon

The President: Thank you all for coming and the family hope you will join them afterwards for Fairtrade coffee and biscuits.

The Dismissal

The President: You may now christen the bride.

All: Whatever.

Offertory Hymn

"I'm getting buried in the morning"

(The collection shall be taken for Dignitas/Relate/Save The Children)

The Duchy of Love

by DAME SYLVIE KRIN, Booker Prize Long Listed (1954)

THE STORY SO FAR: Charles is determined to put a brave face on the inclement summer weather...

"I THOUGHT we could have a picnic, darling. I think it is clearing up."

Charles stood at the leaded French window of the Mountbatten Morning Room, looking at the lowering grey sky outside.

"Don't be daft, Chazza. It's too wet even to go out for a fag." Camilla buried her head in her copy of the *Daily Mail*, freshly ironed by royal aide-de-camp Sir Alan Fitztightly.

"No, you're quite wrong, old thing," Charles persevered. "I can see a patch of blue and by luncheon it'll be bright sunshine, you'll see! I'll get Fitztightly to organise a hamper."

"God, no." Camilla sprang from her chair, throwing aside her paper. "I'll go down to Waitrose in Cirencester and get everything myself."

Charles turned and remonstrated with his beloved. "It's Fitztightly's job, darling. **You** can't be seen wandering around a supermarket with one of those trolley thingies."

"Oh yes, I can, Chazza," Camilla snorted, "and Fitztightly always gets it wrong. Remember when we had the Chief Imam to open the mini mosque in the Islamic Prayer Garden? He brought back two dozen pork pies and a bottle of Scotch."

Charles shrugged, knowing he was defeated and that Camilla would use the opportunity to sneak in a quick fag on the way from her packet of Old Trident Nuclear Strength Naval Shag (untipped).

"You go if you like, but don't forget – support the family business! Duchy Originals!"

"DUCHY Originals? Here they are, Ma'am." The nice lady with the name badge "Vedanta" pointed to a shelf of assorted, tastefully packaged items, all bearing the Royal Crest and the motto *"Organicus Bonus Est"*.

"They are very posh," Vedanta smiled, helpfully.

Camilla surveyed a veritable cornucopia of luxury food items – there were Duchy Basil and Cucumber Biscuits, Duchy Red Pepper Goat Yoghurt, Duchy Beetroot and Gooseberry Marmalade, Duchy Chocolate Nettle Drink and Duchy Cream of Rosehip and Grouse Soup.

And it wasn't only food. Look! There was a garden section. Camilla gasped at the Duchy Gardening Gloves made from sustainable bamboo fibre and imported from Tibet.

"Our hill farmers share our values," she read on the label. And, good grief, a Duchy wind-up hedge trimmer – "The Carbon-Neutral Way To Trim Your Hedge".

Camilla had to remind herself that she was here not to browse but to buy a picnic and Charles was waiting.

She picked up a packet of Duchy Walnut and Carrot Wafers.

"£27.50 for six biscuits?" she exclaimed, reading the price tag. "He must be mad."

Camilla consulted the hovering assistant Vedanta, "Is this right? £27.50?"

"'Fraid so, Ma'am. But we do our own brand for £1.99. And this week they're on special offer..."

"SPECIAL offer!" Charles exploded, as he sat expectantly, cross-legged on the McHackey tartan rug in the middle of the croquet lawn and looked at the packet of biscuits proferred by Camilla. "But these aren't Duchy... they are... er... er... What's the word I'm searching for...? **Appalling**! Yes, that's it. They're appalling! Whatever possessed you to buy them?"

Camilla pointed to the row of bulging plastic bags she had carried out to the picnic spot. "They were cheap! I got the whole caboodle for £15... scotch egg, packet of crisps and a can of coke for 99p! Unbelievable!"

Charles shuddered. "And you brought it all back in those terrible plastic carriers. What happened to the recyclable String Bag For Life that I imported from Botswana?"

"Stop complaining, Chazza," said Camilla, as the first drops of rain began to fall. "The plastic bags will be jolly useful to put on our heads in a few minutes' time."

Charles gazed upward at the dark thunderclouds massing overhead.

Why did everything end up being sort of damp and spoilt?

© Sylvie Krin, Ryanair Holiday Queue Collection

Yes! They are back yet again!

New from the Disaster Catalogue

With holiday in mind...

Gordon is modelling the Out of Office range:

☐ Economic straitjacket
☐ Lost shirt
☐ Trousers with no upturn
☐ Pull-in belt
☐ Scottish brogues

All yours for £2 trillion (payable by your great-grandchildren)

RYANAIR

FOR THE HOLIDAY OF A LIFETIME!

First there was No Frills! Now there is No Flight!

Save pounds when you book a Ryanair holiday. You pay for the flight, but nothing else – because you don't get on it! Beat that for a bargain!!!

Here are some of the destinations you won't be going to:

LIMOGES HELSINKI TIRANA LUND

RYANAIR Not Getting You There For Less!

"You know me, I always read something trashy at the start of the holiday"

BLAIR ON HOLIDAY

I've always fought for the have-yachts

Holiday Range

The 'HULLO SAILOR' collection from Corfu.
The latest in nautical chic!

Peter is wearing a natty Rothschild jacket, Brown slacks (while Peter runs the show!) held up by a black leather belt-up-everybody-else.

A 'shirty shirt' complements the outfit, designed for the man who's in charge (but looks relaxed). A pair of blue loafers (a reference to Cameron and little Osborne!) completes the look.

Gnomewear
It's jolly Boden Weather!

Let's Parlez Franglais!

Numero 94

Un Docteur Français Ecrit

Comme un medecin, je suis often asked, "Docteur, ma femme est tres jolie et tres younger than moi. Elle insiste que je go jogging dans le heat et elle me donne nothing a manger. Regardez, je suis totallement done for! Pardonnez moi, je suis coming over all faint."

Last week, j'ai realised que mon patient etait le President de France est il etait lying unconscious sur le floor.

"Mon Dieu!" j'ai dit. "Je diagnose qu'il sufferit from 'fruity younger wife' syndrome (*Carlabrunius anorexercisiensis abnormalis*, to donner le full nom medicale)."

Qui arrive normalement is que le patient devient plus en plus skinny et puis, phut, il est mort! Quelle tragedy!! Et je have to tell la widow (qui looks tres sexy dressed en noire) que "c'est la vie".

Si vous etes worried that votre jeune femme wants to tuer vous, vous derez consulter un professional avocat de divorce immediatement.

© Le Late Kilometres Kington.

THE RICHARD DAWKINS DARWINIAN SUMMER CAMP

"I'm sorry Cuthbert, but because you came last in the running race... you must die"

Daily Mail

FRIDAY, AUGUST 7, 2009

IT'S RAINING!

Government Warns: Millions Will Get Wet

by Our Weather Staff
Michael Fishfinger

MILLIONS of Britons were shocked yesterday when, without warning, large quantities of water fell out of the sky on top of their heads.

The streets immediately filled with what the Met Office described as "puddles", creating a hazard for motorists, cyclists, pedestrians and other street users.

Health and safety officials warned that old people and toddlers were particularly at risk from this "rain", which is making surfaces slippery and hazardous.

They were advised to stay at home unless their journey was considered "absolutely necessary".

Rain of Terror

Pregnant women were also targeted by Department of Health officials as a specially high-risk group and were advised **not** to get pregnant until the rain had run its course.

The NHS have responded quickly to the rain pandemic by setting up a special "Rainline" to advise members of the public who are worried about the rain.

The helpline received 4 million calls in the first two minutes after it was opened.

Storm In A Teacup

Newly-appointed "rain czar" Lord Sugar announced last night that he will be sending out a 10-page leaflet to every household in the country containing guidelines on how to "stay dry" through the crisis.

Anyone venturing outside while water is still falling out of the sky, the leaflet warns, should take the following safety measures:

- **Wear dedicated protective clothing (eg macintosh, hat, waterproof footwear)**
- **Carry rain-repelling equipment at all times. An "umbrella" (a waterproof version of the familiar parasol or sunshade) can be highly effective, but in cases of emergency it is possible to improvise remedial measures such as a folded newspaper or a Tesco shopping bag.**
- **If in a car or other vehicle, motorists should immediately activate their "windscreen wipers" as rainwater may dangerously impair the driver's vision. Those driving "convertible cars" should "raise the hood" IMMEDIATELY.**
- **Swimmers are advised to get out of the water or they will get wet**
- **The most effective remedy of all against rain is to sing, psychiatrists believe.**

Said one expert yesterday, Dr Jean Kelly from the Hydrotherapy Centre in Poole, "There is no better way to fight off the depression associated with persistent rain than to sing and dance down the street." "This," she said, "will put a smile on your face and make you happy again."

On Other Pages

Will Rain Cause Collapse In House Prices?
Full story and pics **2-94**

MUCH LOVED CARTOON CHARACTER TO BE 'TONED DOWN'

by Our Comic Strip Staff **PC Thomson**

ONE OF Britain's best-loved comic book characters Boris the Johnson is to be given a PC makeover following complaints that he sends the 'wrong signals' to today's youth.

Generations of Britons have revelled in Boris's anarchic sense of mischief and ability to get into scrapes.

With his tousled hair and love of long Latin words, Boris has delighted children of all ages by defying convention with his irreverent antics.

Desperate Dave

But now kill-joy Tory bosses have insisted that Boris clean up his act and present a new caring, compassionate, responsible image more in tune with the new Conservative values of the 21st century.

Out go:
- jokes about watermelons and picaninnies.

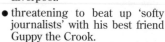

- riding through red lights without a safety helmet.
- poking fun at the 'whingeing scousers' of Liverpool.
- threatening to beat up 'softy journalists' with his best friend Guppy the Crook.
- putting 'Petsy up the duff' and then denying it as a 'pyramid of piffle'.

From now on Boris will be shown with his hair sensibly combed, celebrating London's 'ethnic mix', attending 'Gay Pride' rallies, cycling responsibly in designated cycle lanes and promoting the Olympics as a wonderful opportunity to boost the East London economy. *(That's enough Boring Boris, Ed.)*

BORIS STARS IN EASTENDERS

"Oh, for goodness sake Brian, do you have to be so stoical?"

FREDDIE FAILS IN FINAL TEST

RED BULL SHAME – Where's the booze, Freddie?

by Our Cricketing Staff
Lunchtime O'Val

MILLIONS of cricket lovers were disappointed yesterday by the miserable failure of their all-rounder hero to live up to the nation's expectations as the Ashes series drew to its dramatic climax.

For days, everyone had been looking forward to the moment when "Fantastic Fred" (as no one calls him) would walk off the pitch and proceed to sink 14 bottles of champagne, 24 cognacs and several crates of lager, in celebration of England's historic victory.

Not Out For The Count

Thousands of journalists and photographers had gathered to witness what they hoped would be a final glorious display of Freddie's legendary ability to get drunk.

But it was not to be. Instead of vomiting from the top of a London bus and peeing in the garden of Number Ten, Freddie threw away his big chance for a final moment of glory by tamely choosing instead to go back home to his wife and family.

Middle and Legless

Said one disappointed Flintoff fan, Ken Mumble, "a group of us came up from Sutton Coldfield hoping to see Fred go on a last glorious blinder, which would stand in the record books for ever.

"I tell you, it broke my heart to learn that he was just sitting in a Chinese restaurant with his Dad, eating Dim Sum and sipping mint tea.

"It grieves me to say this, but if that's the best he can do, the game is better without him."

■ *Did Freddie let the nation down? What do you think? Text or email us now on tw@Ivegotnothingelsetodo.com*

An Open Letter To FAY WELDON From Polly Filler

Dear Fay,

We have never met, but I have admired your writing... until now. Fay, love, I have to be honest, your interview in which you said it was okay to pick up your husband's socks and clean the loo let all of us in the sistren down. What could you have been thinking of?

Are you seriously suggesting I should traipse around after the Useless Simon with a toilet brush while he sits slumped in front of the Ashes on Sky Sport, as he has done for what seems like an eternity?

Get real, Fay. It is not my job to pick up his dirties. No, it is the job of the au pair. This week, she happens to come from what used to be a small village in Helmand Province, which Qash-les tells us is now a pile of rubble. So, picking up Useless Simon's pongy socks is scarcely a hardship, compared to picking up the pieces of your grandfather.

So, next time you want to enlighten the world about how women should behave, get your au pair to do it for you.

Yours in the land of sisterhood,

Polly.

Notes & queries

Do wasps go to sleep?

● The answer given by the Rev. Stephen Fieldmouse is only partially correct.

A recent paper from the Institut de Guêpes in Limoges has established that although the wasp may appear to be fully asleep, its condition is more accurately described as 'dozing'. Interestingly the 14th century Florentine poet Gulielmo della Lambretta spoke in one of his sonnets about the 'haply dozing wasp'.

Marjorie Wimpole (Mrs), Dumfries

● Mrs Wimpole makes an all-too familiar mistake when she refers to the "14th century Florentine poet Gulielmo della Lambretta". Not only was he in fact Sienese, but his proper name was Guliemo della Vespa (of the wasp). It was he who gave his name some centuries later to the well-known brand of motor scooter, made popular in Italy in the 1950s by such films as Roman Holiday starring Audrey Hepburn and Cary Grant.

Melanie Wheatcroft (Ms), Hertfordshire

● Ms. Wheatcroft is in error in having Audrey Hepburn as the star of Roman Holiday. The female lead in that rather over-rated 50s comedy was in fact her sister, Katherine Hepburn.

Louis Barfe, Southwold

Answers please to the following:

Who invented the wheelie bin? Can moths whistle? Is it true that the BBC's Radio 3 can be heard on Mars? What is Matthew D'Ancona's real name?

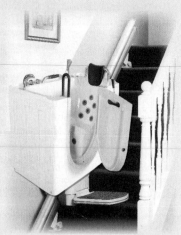

POLICE LOG

Neasden Central Police Station

0847 hrs Armed Response Unit deployed to the St Hazel of Blears Primary School in Poundonly Road, after notification that a Mrs Kirsty Steggles had been causing an affray by complaining to staff that her son Simon had been subjected to alleged bullying by a group of knife-wielding nine-year-olds from nearby Daley Thompson Estate. After assessing the situation, Superintendent Stanmore ordered the tasering of Mrs Steggles at a 50,000-volt level, and she was then taken to the station to be charged with 57 offences under the Wasting Of Police Time Act 2007.

A number of nine-year-olds were offered counselling after suffering the trauma of being falsely accused of bullying.

Social Services took "Child S" (Simon) into care, having assessed his mother as unsuitable to be a parent owing to her obsessive fixation with her son being bullied merely because he came home with occasional multiple stab wounds.

1143 hrs All officers assemble for a Summer Post-Solstitial Ritual Observance since Paganism has now been officially recognised by the Home Office as a bona fide religion, along with Scientology, Moonie-ism, Jedi Warriorism, and C of E.

The High Priestess (WPC Sandra Morden) called on "Beelzebub" to bless the work of the force. A squirrel (grey) was then made the subject of a living sacrifice, after consultation with Health & Safety, in order to ensure good weather for the forthcoming Feast of the Corn Circle, lasting for the duration of the month of August, which will be observed by all Pagan members of the force (everybody) under the orders of the Station Grand Warlock (PC Uxbridge). The station will accordingly be closed until 5 September.

Any members of the public wishing to report a serious crime (e.g. rape, murder, filling the wrong wheelie-bin) are advised to ring Neasden 24/7 Security, a private firm which we can highly recommend as it is run by a number of ex-officers from the Neasden station who have retired early for reasons of ill-health.

School news

St Cakes

Retake Term begins today. There are 20,968 pupils in the school. A.J.R. Short-Planke (Dimmers) remains Head of Scholars until a university place becomes available. Miss Fruitella Aire-Head (Yahs) is still Senior Girl pending the re-mark of her Reality TV A-level and her acceptance by the University of Raynes Park (formerly The World of Sofas). Five new Houses are in the process of construction on Ploughman's Lunch Meadow to accommodate the increased number of students. They will be named after recent benefactors of the school – Emirates, GazProm, Manchester City, The Chinese Communist Party, Lakeland. St Cakes Day will be celebrated on November 5th when Sir Fred Goodwin (O.C) will speak on the theme of "A Second Career: The Challenge of the Post-Recession Landscape". He will then formally close the computer centre. There will be a performance of Pirandello's *Six Characters in Search of a Place at Leeds* on 5th December. Tickets from the bursar Major Ecclestone, The Pits. The Run will be held on The Bank on 11th October. Bailouts are on December 12th.

 How They Are Not Related Any More

The Divorce Of The Century

Zachariah	Rimsky-Korsakov
St John The Baptist	Princess Sheherezade
St James The Fishpaste	Ali Baba
Sir Jammy Goldfinger	Babar The Elephant
Blofeld	Lyn Babar (of the Observer)
Oddjob	Lord Rothschild
Sir Jaws Goldsmith	Mouton Dressed As Rothschild
Lady Annabel Fishpaste (née Puddleduck)	Lord Mandelson
Jemima Fishpaste	David Cameron
Zac Marmite	**Sherezac Fishpaste**

"Still copying the Beatles, then"

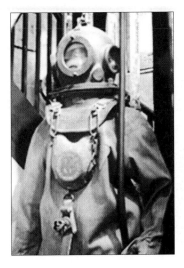

EDWARD KENNEDY DIES

What do you think your legacy will be?

We'll cross that bridge when we come to it

WORLD MOURNS 'GREATEST EVER STATESMAN'

by Our Entire Staff

THEY ARE calling him "the greatest statesman of our time". The mark he has left on the history of our age will never be erased.

Today, with the departure of the man known to millions as simply Senator Edward Kennedy, mankind has lost one of its finest sons.

One of his greatest achievements was to be the brother of President John F. Kennedy, so cruelly assassinated in 1963.

But he did more. He was also the brother of Robert Kennedy, so cruelly assassinated in 1968.

Jolly Good Chappaquiddick

But possibly his greatest achievement was to rebuild his career following the tragic accident at Chappaquiddick in 1969, in which he was so unfortunate as to be involved.

How did he do it? The answer is simple. It was a tribute to the fact that he was not only the brother of former President Kennedy, but also the brother of Robert Kennedy.

Those Kennedy funeral arrangements in full

1pm
Hearse carrying Edward Kennedy's body leaves the church to begin the three miles drive to the cemetery.

1.13pm
Hearse inexplicably speeds up in heavy fog as it approaches rickety bridge.

1.14pm
Hearse careers of the bridge and crashes into the icy water of the lake below.

1.19pm
Hearse driver panics and runs off.

Nine hours later
Hearse driver turns up in Connecticut and Edward Kennedy's coffin is finally reported missing.

NEW EDITOR OF THE SUN REVEALED

Old Editor

New Editor

That Alan Yentob BBC Xmas Lunch On Expenses Menu in full

Series of Turkeys with Plenty of Gravy

– ✳ –

Beard and Butter-Up Pudding

– ✳ –

To Drink: *Botney's Red Barrel*

(That's enough Menu. Ed)

BBC Radio 3

Opera Highlights

The Damnation Of Silvio
by Hector Berliozsconi

AS the curtain rises, we see the Robber Baron Silvio hosting a lavish banquet at the Palazzo Copulazzione. He is surrounded by a chorus of beautiful young women, many of whom are members of the European Parliament. They are singing the famous Rumpipumpi Chorus from the popular operetta *Orgy And Bess*.

But their merrymaking is interrupted by the arrival of the Baron's stern but beautiful daughter, Barbara. She rebukes him in the moving aria *Che bastardo lei* ("O Father, you are guilty of inappropriate behaviour").

The Baron is unmoved and dismisses her, saying "Mamma mia" ("You're worse than your mother").

But, as the festivities recommence, there is a clap of thunder and we see His Holiness the Pope arriving in his Popemobile, flanked by a chorus of Cardinals on motorbikes wearing red helmets and dark glasses. He addresses the Baron in his native German, singing the fearsome *Schweinhund* aria, beginning with the curse "Gotterdammerung" ("God damn you, you lascivious lecher, you will go to hell").

Just as we expect Silvio to be dragged down to the underworld by demons, a chorus of Italian voters enters and carries him shoulder-high to his favourite brothel.

The Pope sadly withdraws, and they sing triumphantly "Papa gono" ("His Holiness has left the building").

(CURTAIN)

"I hate to see spelling mistakes"

£££ *Charity Appeal* £££

ALAN, seen above, has suffered for years from Touries Syndrome, which leads him to swear uncontrollably and to complain that he is being persecuted. So bad has this affliction recently become that poor Alan is now in danger of losing his job. When he was secretly filmed in the House of Commons using a well-known expletive, this appeared on the front page of the *Daily Telegraph*. Alan, a multi-millionaire, then rambled on incoherently about having to live on 'rations' and claimed that the whole world apart from himself had "gone mad".

Researchers claim that Alan's case is a particularly acute example of an affliction which has lately struck down many MPs, as they face up to the harsh reality of having to live without fiddling their expenses.

Please send money now.

● £2,000 will provide Alan with the services of a part-time gardener.

● £10,000 will provide him with an agreeable lunch at the Manoir de Quatre Matelots.

● £1,000,000 will buy Alan a life-peerage under the Cameron Government.

Send you contribution now to the Touries Syndrome Society, The Old Fuckhouse *(surely Duckhouse? Ed.)*, Shittingbourne, Kent.

Cluff

A Taxi Driver writes

EVERY week a well-known cabbie is invited to comment on an issue of topical importance. This week **Normo Tebbs** (cab no. 4372856) on the future of the Conservative Party.

What d'you reckon to that Cameron, guv? If you ask me, he's useless! I mean, with the old Tories you knew where you stood – Enoch, Maggie... you wouldn't catch *her* going on holiday wearing shorts and a polo shirt, no, nowadays you'd be better off voting for the UKIP lot. Very clever men – Europe, immigration, immigration, Europe, immigration, immigration... No, them UKIP they talk a lot of sense. That David Cameron, though, he's rubbish!

Oi! There's that bloody Boris on a bike! They shouldn't be allowed in the bus lanes, should they? Let's run him over! Ha! Ha! Ha! I 'ad that Kilroy Silk in the back of the cab once. A *real* gentleman...

Normo Tebbs's new book How To Cook Cameron's Goose *is published by Snipcook & Feed, £19.99.*

BURMA VERDICT – HOUSE ARREST EXTENDED

Aung San Suu Kyi – you are found guilty of reason

New Movies

Shred II

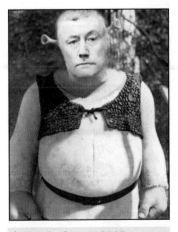

He's back! The return of the unloveable ogre who fled to France with his pot of gold after his accounts were revealed to be fairy tales.

Now Shred is back with a whole new adventure.

First, Fred needs a job, but he has to convince everyone that he isn't just a scary monster who makes everyone run to the banks and take out their money as soon as he appears!

Can Shred turn into Prince Charming and start a new life?

★ **Eye Rating: ££££££.**

Voice of Shred	**Gordon Brown**
Voice of Donkey	**Alistair Darling**
Voice of Fairy Godmother	**Harriet Harman**
Voice of Reason	**Vince Cable**

BROWN AND OUT!

BANKER ROW SPLITS LABOUR

STRIKES: BROWN'S PLEDGE

COMIC RELIEF
Gordon sucks up to celebrities

BROWN MEETS POPE

SWINE FLU ADVICE

GORDON AND THE KIDS

BROWN MEETS GADDAFI

Economy under threat

Freedom under threat

THEY THINK IT'S ALL OVER